# Cooking for Two

Taste of Home® BOOKS

**RDA ENTHUSIAST BRANDS, LLC**
**MILWAUKEE, WI**

# Taste of Home

**EDITORIAL**
**EDITOR-IN-CHIEF** Catherine Cassidy
**VICE PRESIDENT, CONTENT OPERATIONS** Kerri Balliet
**CREATIVE DIRECTOR** Howard Greenberg

**MANAGING EDITOR, PRINT & DIGITAL BOOKS** Mark Hagen
**ASSOCIATE CREATIVE DIRECTOR** Edwin Robles Jr.

**EDITOR** Hazel Wheaton
**ART DIRECTOR** Maggie Conners
**LAYOUT DESIGNER** Nancy Novak
**EDITORIAL SERVICES MANAGER** Dena Ahlers
**EDITORIAL PRODUCTION COORDINATOR** Jill Banks
**COPY CHIEF** Deb Warlaumont Mulvey
**COPY EDITORS** Dulcie Shoener (senior), Ronald Kovach,
Chris McLaughlin, Ellie Piper
**CONTRIBUTING COPY EDITORS** Michael Juley, Valerie Phillips

**CONTENT DIRECTOR** Julie Blume Benedict
**FOOD EDITORS** Gina Nistico; James Schend;
Peggy Woodward, RDN
**RECIPE EDITORS** Sue Ryon (lead), Irene Yeh
**EDITORIAL SERVICES ADMINISTRATOR** Marie Brannon

**CULINARY DIRECTOR** Sarah Thompson
**TEST COOKS** Nicholas Iverson (lead), Matthew Hass
**FOOD STYLISTS** Kathryn Conrad (lead), Lauren Knoelke,
Shannon Roum
**PREP COOKS** Bethany Van Jacobson (lead), Melissa Hansen,
Aria C. Thornton
**CULINARY TEAM ASSISTANT** Maria Petrella

**PHOTOGRAPHY DIRECTOR** Stephanie Marchese
**PHOTOGRAPHERS** Dan Roberts, Jim Wieland
**PHOTOGRAPHER/SET STYLIST** Grace Natoli Sheldon
**SET STYLISTS** Melissa Franco (lead), Stacey Genaw,
Dee Dee Schaefer
**SET STYLIST ASSISTANT** Stephanie Chojnacki

**BUSINESS ARCHITECT, PUBLISHING TECHNOLOGIES**
Amanda Harmatys
**BUSINESS ANALYST, PUBLISHING TECHNOLOGIES** Kate Unger
**JUNIOR BUSINESS ANALYST, PUBLISHING TECHNOLOGIES**
Shannon Stroud

**EDITORIAL BUSINESS MANAGER** Kristy Martin
**RIGHTS & PERMISSIONS ASSOCIATE** Samantha Lea Stoeger
**EDITORIAL BUSINESS ASSOCIATE** Andrea Meiers

**EDITOR, *TASTE OF HOME*** Emily Betz Tyra
**ART DIRECTOR, *TASTE OF HOME*** Kristin Bowker

**BUSINESS**
**VICE PRESIDENT, GROUP PUBLISHER** Kirsten Marchioli
**PUBLISHER, *TASTE OF HOME*** Donna Lindskog
**BUSINESS DEVELOPMENT DIRECTOR, TASTE OF HOME LIVE**
Laurel Osman
**STRATEGIC PARTNERSHIPS MANAGER, TASTE OF HOME LIVE**
Jamie Piette Andrzejewski

**TRUSTED MEDIA BRANDS, INC.**
**PRESIDENT & CHIEF EXECUTIVE OFFICER** Bonnie Kintzer
**CHIEF FINANCIAL OFFICER** Dean Durbin
**CHIEF MARKETING OFFICER** C. Alec Casey
**CHIEF REVENUE OFFICER** Richard Sutton
**CHIEF DIGITAL OFFICER** Vince Errico
**SENIOR VICE PRESIDENT, GLOBAL HR & COMMUNICATIONS**
Phyllis E. Gebhardt, SPHR; SHRM-SCP
**GENERAL COUNSEL** Mark Sirota
**VICE PRESIDENT, PRODUCT MARKETING** Brian Kennedy
**VICE PRESIDENT, OPERATIONS** Michael Garzone
**VICE PRESIDENT, CONSUMER MARKETING PLANNING** Jim Woods
**VICE PRESIDENT, DIGITAL PRODUCT & TECHNOLOGY**
Nick Contardo
**VICE PRESIDENT, FINANCIAL PLANNING & ANALYSIS**
William Houston

FOR OTHER *TASTE OF HOME* BOOKS AND PRODUCTS,
visit us at **tasteofhome.com.**

**INTERNATIONAL STANDARD BOOK NUMBER** 978-1-61765-650-7
**LIBRARY OF CONGRESS CONTROL NUMBER** 2017930994

**PICTURED ON FRONT COVER** Salmon Salad with Glazed Walnuts,
page 229; Chicken Gyros, page 109; Mixed Fruit Shortcakes, page 285;
Chicken Reuben Roll-Ups, page 195

**PICTURED ON TITLE PAGE** Chocolate Lava Cakes, page 302

**PICTURED ON BACK COVER** Tender 'n' Tangy Ribs, page 203;
Rustic Fruit Tart, page 297

**Printed in China**
1 3 5 7 9 10 8 6 4 2

SANTA FE CHICKEN
PITA PIZZAS, 191

GARDEN CHICKPEA
SALAD, 120

CILANTRO BEAN
BURGERS, 106

CITRUS CREAM
TARTLETS, 301

# CONTENTS

To find a recipe tasteofhome.com
To submit a recipe tasteofhome.com/submit
To find out about other *Taste of Home* products
shoptasteofhome.com

 LIKE US
facebook.com/
tasteofhome

 TWEET US
twitter.com/tasteofhome

 FOLLOW US
@tasteofhome

 PIN US
pinterest.com/taste_of_home

SAUCY BEEF WITH BROCCOLI, 159

# Share a **Home-Cooked** Meal Tonight!

**Small households deserve fresh home-cooked meals, too! Forget prepackaged meals or endless leftovers—Taste of Home Cooking for Two presents 141 of the best recipes that today's cooks turn to when creating great meals for a pair!**

Between recipes with a too-large yield and shopping trips with a too-large haul, it's easy to waste money, waste food or inflate portion sizes when cooking for a pair. This indispensable collection lets you make the meal you want in just the size you need! **Breakfast dishes, appetizers, soups** and **sandwiches, side dishes, entrees** of all kinds, and **desserts**—all perfectly portioned for two.

CHICKEN CHILI ENCHILADAS, 184

## Look for these handy icons for quick meal planning:

**EAT SMART**

Lighten up your meals by trimming back on calories, fat, carbs and/or sodium.

**FAST FIX**

Make a great meal in record time with these under-30-minute recipes!

**(5) INGREDIENTS**

Keep it simple with recipes that take only five ingredients (not including salt, pepper, oil and water, or optional extras).

These great recipes make it simple to create fresh, delicious meals that won't leave you with a fridge full of leftovers. All of the recipes were tested in the *Taste of Home* **Test Kitchen,** so you know they'll turn out just right.

The **large-print format** means that you'll never struggle to read measurements, and **a full-color photo with every recipe** makes the step-by-step instructions even clearer.

Crack open **Cooking for Two** and get started today!

OMELET CROISSANTS, 20

**Fluffy Pumpkin Pancakes, p. 12**

# Breakfast for Two

Whether it's a weekend brunch or a weekday morning engine-starter, think outside the cereal box when it comes to breakfast!

**Hearty Sausage 'n' Hash Browns, p. 11**

**Peanut Butter Oatmeal, p. 31**

**Individual Italian Frittatas, p. 16**

**FAST FIX** ▶

# Fruit-Filled French Toast Wraps

If you need a lovely dish for breakfast or brunch, these tortilla wraps made like French toast are chock-full of fruity goodness and granola.

—**DAWN JARVIS** BRECKENRIDGE, MN

**START TO FINISH:** 25 MIN.
**MAKES:** 2 SERVINGS

¾  cup (6 ounces) vanilla yogurt
⅔  cup sliced ripe banana
1  large egg
¼  cup 2% milk
1  teaspoon ground cinnamon
½  teaspoon ground nutmeg
2  whole wheat tortillas (8 inches)
2  teaspoons butter
⅔  cup sliced fresh strawberries
⅔  cup fresh blueberries
¼  cup granola
    Confectioners' sugar (optional)

**1.** In a small bowl, combine yogurt and banana. In a shallow bowl, whisk egg, milk, cinnamon and nutmeg. Dip both sides of each tortilla in the egg mixture. In a skillet, heat butter over medium-high heat. Add the tortilla; cook for 1-2 minutes on each side or until golden brown.

**2.** Spoon the yogurt mixture down the center of the tortillas, then top it with strawberries, blueberries and granola. Roll up each tortilla; if desired, dust with confectioners' sugar or finish with dollop of yogurt and more fruit and granola.

**NUTRITION FACTS** 1 wrap equals 399 cal., 10 g fat (4 g sat. fat), 72 mg chol., 256 mg sodium, 68 g carb. (29 g sugars, 9 g fiber), 15 g pro.

**TOP TIP**

This recipe is perfect to play with! Try different combinations of fresh fruit and flavors of yogurt. Granola comes in many varieties as well. You can even vary the spices you use to flavor the tortillas—try ginger or cardamom.

# Hearty Sausage 'n' Hash Browns

Turn frozen hash browns into a satisfying meal by adding smoked sausage and green peppers. It's an uncomplicated dish that works any time of day.

**—VIOLET BEARD** MARSHALL, IL

---

**START TO FINISH:** 30 MIN.
**MAKES:** 3 SERVINGS

---

4   cups frozen cubed hash brown potatoes
¼   cup chopped green pepper
⅓   cup canola oil
¼   pound smoked sausage, halved lengthwise and cut into ¼-inch slices
3   slices process American cheese

In a large skillet, cook potatoes and pepper in oil over medium heat until the potatoes are golden brown. Stir in sausage; heat through. Remove from heat; top with cheese. Cover and let stand for 5 minutes or until the cheese is melted.

**NUTRITION FACTS** 1 cup equals 477 cal., 39 g fat (11 g sat. fat), 39 mg chol., 695 mg sodium, 21 g carb. (3 g sugars, 2 g fiber), 12 g pro.

# Fluffy Pumpkin Pancakes

My daughters love these tender, fluffy pancakes served with butter, syrup and whipped cream.

**—MINDY BAUKNECHT** TWO RIVERS, WI

---

**PREP:** 15 MIN. • **COOK:** 10 MIN./BATCH
**MAKES:** 6 PANCAKES

---

⅓ cup all-purpose flour
⅓ cup whole wheat flour
2 tablespoons sugar
½ teaspoon baking powder
½ teaspoon baking soda
¼ teaspoon pumpkin pie spice
⅛ teaspoon ground cinnamon
   Dash salt
1 large egg
½ cup fat-free milk
⅓ cup vanilla yogurt
⅓ cup canned pumpkin
1 tablespoon canola oil
⅛ teaspoon vanilla extract
   Maple syrup

**1.** In a bowl, whisk together the first eight ingredients. In another bowl, whisk the next six ingredients until blended. Add to dry ingredients; stir just until moistened.

**2.** Lightly coat a griddle with cooking spray, then preheat over medium heat. Pour the batter by ⅓ cupfuls onto the griddle. Cook until the bubbles on top begin to pop. Turn; cook until golden brown. Serve with syrup.

**NUTRITION FACTS** 3 pancakes (calculated without syrup) equals 360 cal., 11 g fat (2 g sat. fat), 109 mg chol., 579 mg sodium, 55 g carb. (23 g sugars, 5 g fiber), 13 g pro.

**DID YOU KNOW?**

Pancakes freeze well, so if you do have any leftovers (unlikely, but possible!), wrap them in plastic and put them in the freezer. The next time you want a delicious breakfast, just zap them in the microwave.

# Spinach-Mushroom Scrambled Eggs

After my husband and I enjoyed a mushroom-egg dish at a hotel restaurant, I created a healthy version with loads of hearty mushroom flavor.

**—RACHELLE MCCALLA** BATESVILLE, AR

**START TO FINISH:** 15 MIN.
**MAKES:** 2 SERVINGS

- 2 large eggs
- 2 large egg whites
- 1/8 teaspoon salt
- 1/8 teaspoon pepper
- 1 teaspoon butter
- 1/2 cup thinly sliced fresh mushrooms
- 1/2 cup fresh baby spinach, chopped
- 2 tablespoons shredded provolone cheese

**1.** In a small bowl, whisk eggs, egg whites, salt and pepper until blended. In a small nonstick skillet, heat butter over medium-high heat. Add mushrooms; cook and stir for 3-4 minutes or until tender. Add spinach; cook and stir until wilted. Reduce heat to medium.

**2.** Add the egg mixture; cook and stir just until the eggs are thickened and no liquid egg remains. Stir in cheese.

**NUTRITION FACTS** 1 serving equals 162 cal., 11 g fat (5 g sat. fat), 226 mg chol., 417 mg sodium, 2 g carb. (1 g sugars, 0 fiber), 14 g pro. *Diabetic Exchanges:* 2 medium-fat meat.

# Individual Italian Frittatas

The Italian word "frittata" refers to frying an egg-based dish in a skillet. This version with added salami, roasted sweet pepper and mozzarella is baked in a ramekin but the ending is the same—delicious, day or night.

**—NANCY ELLIOTT** HOUSTON, TX

**PREP:** 25 MIN. • **BAKE:** 20 MIN.
**MAKES:** 2 SERVINGS

- ¼ cup finely chopped onion
- 2 teaspoons olive oil
- 4 medium fresh mushrooms, chopped
- 4 thin slices hard salami, julienned
- 2 tablespoons finely chopped roasted sweet red pepper
- 4 large eggs
- 1 tablespoon 2% milk
- 1 tablespoon grated Parmesan cheese
- 2 teaspoons minced fresh parsley
- 1 teaspoon minced fresh chives
  Dash pepper
- ¼ cup shredded part-skim mozzarella cheese
  Chopped fresh chives, optional

**1.** In a small skillet, cook and stir onion in oil over medium heat until tender. Add mushrooms; cook 2-4 minutes longer or until tender. Divide between two greased 8-ounce ramekins. Top with salami and red pepper.

**2.** In a small bowl, whisk eggs, milk, Parmesan cheese, parsley, minced chives and pepper; pour into ramekins. Bake at 400° for 10 minutes.

**3.** Sprinkle witwlla cheese; bake 8-10 minutes longer or until eggs are set. Sprinkle with chopped chives if desired.

**NUTRITION FACTS** 1 ramekin equals 339 cal., 24 g fat (8 g sat. fat), 456 mg chol., 751 mg sodium, 6 g carb. (3 g sugars, 1 g fiber), 24 g pro.

**TOP TIP**

Feel free to experiment with this recipe! The basic process is the same; cook any vegetables until they are tender before putting them in the ramekins. If you're using meat, make sure it's precooked, or cook it until it's no longer pink.

# Vanilla French Toast

We discovered this recipe in Mexico. We couldn't figure out what made this French toast so delicious until we learned the secret was vanilla—one of Mexico's most popular flavorings. Since then, we've added a touch of vanilla to our waffle and pancake recipes. It makes them all very tasty.

**—JOE AND BOBBI SCHOTT** CASTROVILLE, TX

**START TO FINISH:** 10 MIN.
**MAKES:** 2 SERVINGS

- 2 large eggs
- 1/2 cup 2% milk
- 1 tablespoon sugar
- 1 teaspoon vanilla extract
  Pinch salt
- 6 slices day-old bread
  Maple syrup or cinnamon sugar

In a shallow bowl, beat eggs; add milk, sugar, vanilla and salt. Soak bread for 30 seconds on each side. Cook on a greased hot griddle until golden brown on both sides and cooked through. Serve with syrup or cinnamon sugar.

**NUTRITION FACTS** 3 slices equals 332 cal., 11 g fat (4 g sat. fat), 218 mg chol., 558 mg sodium, 44 g carb. (14 g sugars, 2 g fiber), 14 g pro.

FAST FIX

## Omelet Croissants

Bacon and eggs never tasted so good, stacked with cheese, greens, tomato and more in this grilled meal-in-one.
—**EDNA COBURN** TUCSON, AZ

**START TO FINISH:** 30 MIN.
**MAKES:** 2 SERVINGS

- 3 large eggs
- 1 tablespoon water
- 1 teaspoon chicken bouillon granules
- 1 green onion, finely chopped
- 2 tablespoons finely chopped sweet red pepper
- 1/4 teaspoon lemon-pepper seasoning
- 1/2 teaspoon butter
- 2 croissants, split
- 4 1/2 teaspoons ranch salad dressing
- 4 slices Canadian bacon
- 4 slices Muenster cheese
- 1/2 cup fresh arugula
- 4 thin slices tomato

**1.** In a small bowl, whisk eggs, water and bouillon; set aside.

**2.** In a small nonstick skillet over medium heat, cook onion, red pepper and lemon pepper in butter until tender.

**3.** Add the egg mixture. As the eggs set, push the cooked edges toward the center, letting the uncooked portion flow underneath. When the eggs are completely set, fold the omelet in half and cut into two wedges.

**4.** Spread croissants with salad dressing. On the croissant bottoms, layer bacon, omelet, cheese, arugula and tomato. Replace croissant tops.

**5.** Cook on a panini maker or indoor grill for 2-4 minutes or until cheese is melted.

**NUTRITION FACTS** 1 serving equals 667 cal., 43 g fat (20 g sat. fat), 427 mg chol., 2099 mg sodium, 32 g carb. (10 g sugars, 2 g fiber), 36 g pro.

# Breakfast Burritos

Eating on the run? Get up and out the door with these hearty handhelds.

**—JENNY WHITE** GLEN, MS

---

**START TO FINISH:** 30 MIN.
**MAKES:** 2 SERVINGS

---

- 2 ounces bulk pork sausage
- 2 large eggs
- 2 tablespoons chopped tomato
- 2 tablespoons chopped onion
- 2 teaspoons canned chopped green chilies
   Dash pepper
- 2 slices process American cheese
- 2 flour tortillas (10 inches), warmed
- 3 tablespoons salsa
- 3 tablespoons sour cream

**1.** In a large skillet, cook the sausage over medium heat until no longer pink; drain. In a large bowl, whisk the eggs, tomato, onion, chilies and pepper. Add to the skillet; cook and stir until set.

**2.** Place a cheese slice on each tortilla. Spoon the filling off-center onto each tortilla. Top with salsa and sour cream. Fold the sides and ends of the tortilla over the filling and roll up.

**NUTRITION FACTS** 1 serving equals 464 cal., 23 g fat (10 g sat. fat), 250 mg chol., 943 mg sodium, 37 g carb. (4 g sugars, 6 g fiber), 19 g pro.

EAT SMART **FAST FIX**

## Flaxseed Oatmeal Pancakes

I came up with this tasty recipe because my husband loves pancakes and I wanted a healthier option. They have a pleasing texture and a delightful touch of cinnamon.

**—SHARON HANSEN** PONTIAC, IL

**START TO FINISH:** 20 MIN.
**MAKES:** 4 PANCAKES

- 1/3  cup whole wheat flour
- 3    tablespoons quick-cooking oats
- 1    tablespoon flaxseed
- 1/2  teaspoon baking powder
- 1/4  teaspoon ground cinnamon
- 1/8  teaspoon baking soda
       Dash salt
- 1    large egg, separated
- 1/2  cup buttermilk
- 1    tablespoon brown sugar
- 1    tablespoon canola oil
- 1/2  teaspoon vanilla extract

**1.** In a large bowl, combine the first seven ingredients. In a small bowl, whisk the egg yolk, buttermilk, brown sugar, oil and vanilla; stir into the dry ingredients just until moistened.

**2.** In a small bowl, beat egg white on medium speed until stiff peaks form. Fold into the batter.

**3.** Pour the batter by 1/4 cupfuls onto a hot griddle coated with cooking spray; turn when bubbles form on top. Cook until the second side is golden brown.

**NUTRITION FACTS** 2 pancakes equals 273 cal., 13 g fat (2 g sat. fat), 108 mg chol., 357 mg sodium, 31 g carb. (10 g sugars, 5 g fiber), 10 g pro. *Diabetic Exchanges:* 2 starch, 2 fat.

**TOP TIP**

To make restaurant-style whipped butter for your pancakes, let the butter soften at room temperature, then beat it with an electric mixer until it's light and fluffy. Try mixing in a little honey, confectioners' sugar or orange zest for added flavor.

# Camembert Souffles

Set the mood for a romantic morning meal with these beautiful souffles. They can help make an ordinary morning special.

—**IRINA UMMEL** ARLINGTON, WA

---

**PREP:** 30 MIN. • **BAKE:** 20 MIN.
**MAKES:** 2 SERVINGS

---

2   large egg whites
2   tablespoons grated
     Parmesan cheese
1   tablespoon butter
2¼  teaspoons all-purpose flour
     Dash ground nutmeg
     Dash cayenne pepper
½   cup 2% milk
⅓   cup shredded Gruyere
     or Swiss cheese
1   ounce Camembert cheese
1½  teaspoons sherry or reduced-
     sodium chicken broth
½   teaspoon Dijon mustard
1   large egg yolk, lightly beaten
     Dash cream of tartar
     Dash salt

**1.** Let egg whites stand at room temperature for 30 minutes. Coat two 8-oz. ramekins with cooking spray and lightly sprinkle with Parmesan cheese; set aside.

**2.** In a small saucepan, melt butter. Whisk in flour, nutmeg and cayenne until smooth; gradually add milk. Bring to a boil over medium heat; cook and stir for 2 minutes or until thickened. Reduce heat; stir in the Gruyere, Camembert, sherry and mustard until the cheeses are melted. Remove from heat. Transfer to a small bowl.

**3.** Stir a small amount of the hot mixture into egg yolk; return all to the bowl, stirring constantly. Allow to cool slightly.

**4.** In a small bowl with clean beaters, beat egg whites, cream of tartar and salt until stiff peaks form. With a spatula, fold egg whites into cheese mixture until combined. Transfer to prepared ramekins.

**5.** Bake at 375° for 18-22 minutes or until the tops are puffed and centers appear set. Serve immediately.

**NUTRITION FACTS** 1 ramekin equals 253 cal., 17 g fat (10 g sat. fat), 149 mg chol., 497 mg sodium, 7 g carb. (4 g sugars, 0 fiber), 17 g pro.

## Southwest Tortilla Scramble

Here's my version of a deconstructed breakfast burrito that's actually good for you. Go for hefty corn tortillas in this recipe—flour ones can get lost in the scramble.

—**CHRISTINE SCHENHER** EXETER, CA

**START TO FINISH:** 15 MIN.
**MAKES:** 2 SERVINGS

- 4 large egg whites
- 2 large eggs
- ¼ teaspoon pepper
- 2 corn tortillas (6 inches), halved and cut into strips
- ¼ cup chopped fresh spinach
- 2 tablespoons shredded reduced-fat cheddar cheese
- ¼ cup salsa

**1.** In a large bowl, whisk egg whites, eggs and pepper. Stir in tortillas, spinach and cheese.

**2.** Heat a large skillet coated with cooking spray over medium heat. Pour in the egg mixture; cook and stir until the eggs are thickened and no liquid egg remains. Top with salsa.

**NUTRITION FACTS** 1 serving equals 195 cal., 7 g fat (3 g sat. fat), 217 mg chol., 391 mg sodium, 16 g carb. (2 g sugars, 2 g fiber), 17 g pro. *Diabetic Exchanges:* 2 lean meat, 1 starch.

## Peanut Butter Oatmeal

My son and I eat this every day. It is truly a hearty, healthy breakfast to jump-start our day.

**—ELISABETH REITENBACH** TERRYVILLE, CT

**START TO FINISH:** 15 MIN.
**MAKES:** 2 SERVINGS

1¾  cups water
⅛  teaspoon salt
1  cup old-fashioned oats
2  tablespoons creamy peanut butter
2  tablespoons honey
2  teaspoons ground flaxseed
½  to 1 teaspoon ground cinnamon
    Chopped apple, optional

In a small saucepan, bring water and salt to a boil. Stir in oats; cook for 5 minutes over medium heat, stirring occasionally. Transfer the oatmeal to bowls; stir in peanut butter, honey, flaxseed, cinnamon and, if desired, apple. Serve immediately.

**NUTRITION FACTS** ¾ cup (calculated without apple) equals 323 cal., 12 g fat (2 g sat. fat), 0 chol., 226 mg sodium, 49 g carb. (19 g sugars, 6 g fiber), 11 g pro.

**Smoked Turkey Pizza, p. 40**

# Appetizers for Two

Looking for snacks, starters or small-plate suppers? This chapter offers great choices that range from easy to impressive.

**Refreshing Tomato Bruschetta, p. 47**

**Dill Spiral Bites, p. 36**

**Beef Nachos Supreme, p. 48**

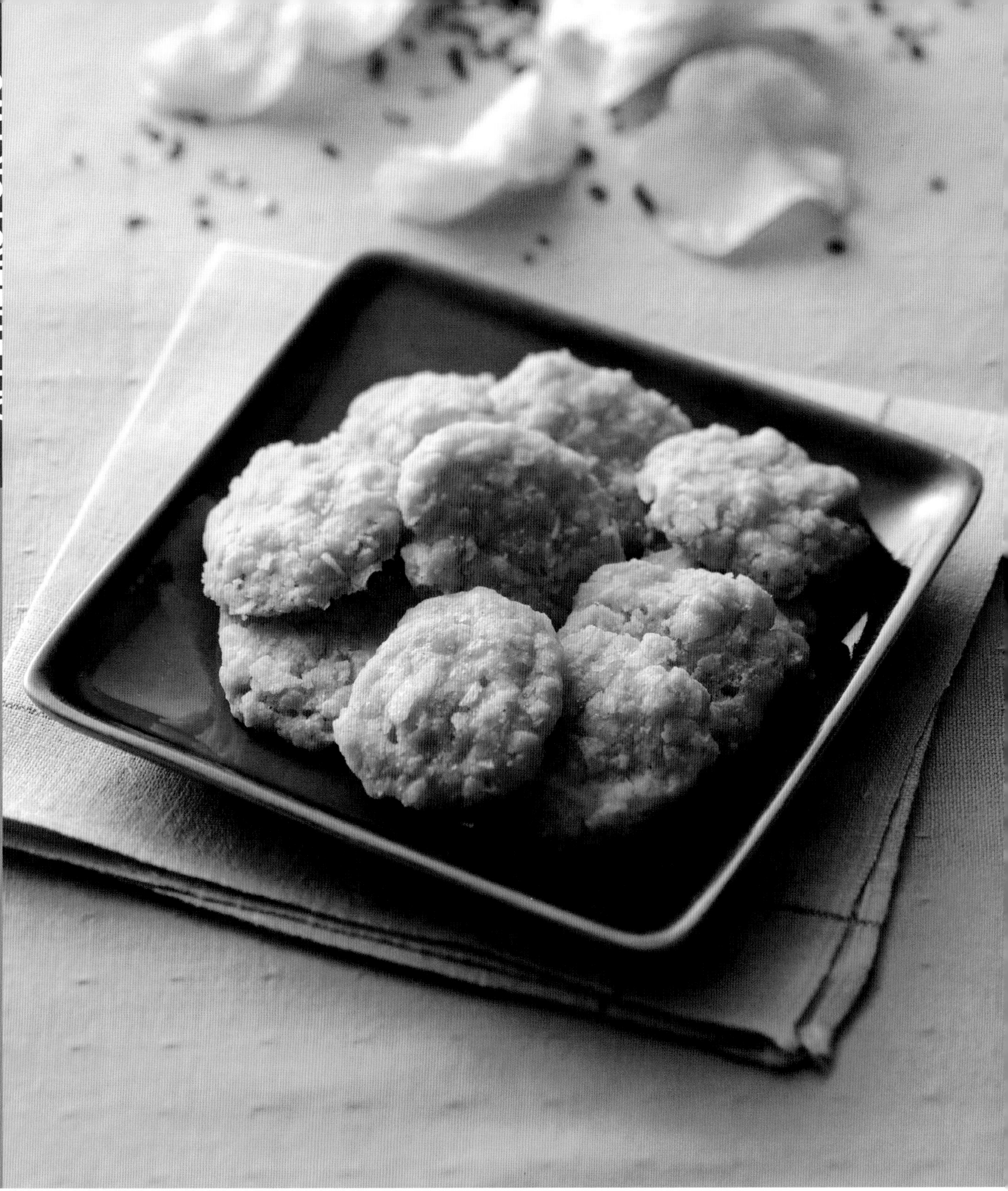

# Crunchy Cheese Crisps

I bake these zesty appetizers for a nearby bed-and-breakfast. They go together in minutes, and guests never seem able to stop with just one.

**—CAROL GRASBY** STRATFORD, ON

**START TO FINISH:** 20 MIN.
**MAKES:** 2 SERVINGS

- ¼ cup finely crushed potato chips
- ¼ cup finely shredded cheddar cheese
- 2 tablespoons all-purpose flour
- 1 tablespoon butter, softened
- ¼ teaspoon Dijon mustard
  Pinch cayenne pepper

In a small bowl, combine all ingredients. Shape into ¾-in. balls. Place on an ungreased baking sheet and flatten slightly. Bake at 350° for 8-10 minutes or until golden brown. Remove to a wire rack.

**NUTRITION FACTS** 4 crisps equals 167 cal., 12 g fat (7 g sat. fat), 30 mg chol., 200 mg sodium, 10 g carb. (0 sugars, 1 g fiber), 4 g pro. *Diabetic Exchanges:* 2½ fat, ½ starch.

# Dill Spiral Bites

It takes only six ingredients to roll out these savory pinwheels. They're great for lunch, as a snack or with soup.
—**VALERIE BELLEY** ST. LOUIS, MO

**PREP:** 15 MIN. + CHILLING
**MAKES:** 2 SERVINGS

- 1 package (3 ounces) cream cheese, softened
- 1 tablespoon minced chives
- 1 tablespoon snipped fresh dill
- 2 flour tortillas (8 inches)
- 6 thin slices tomato
- 6 large spinach leaves

**1.** In a small bowl, beat cream cheese, chives and dill until blended. Spread about 1 tablespoonful over one side of each tortilla. Layer with tomato and spinach; spread with the remaining cream cheese mixture.

**2.** Roll up each tortilla tightly; wrap in plastic. Refrigerate for at least 1 hour. Unwrap and cut each into four slices.

**NUTRITION FACTS** 4 slices equals 271 cal., 12 g fat (6 g sat. fat), 30 mg chol., 458 mg sodium, 31 g carb. (3 g sugars, 2 g fiber), 10 g pro.

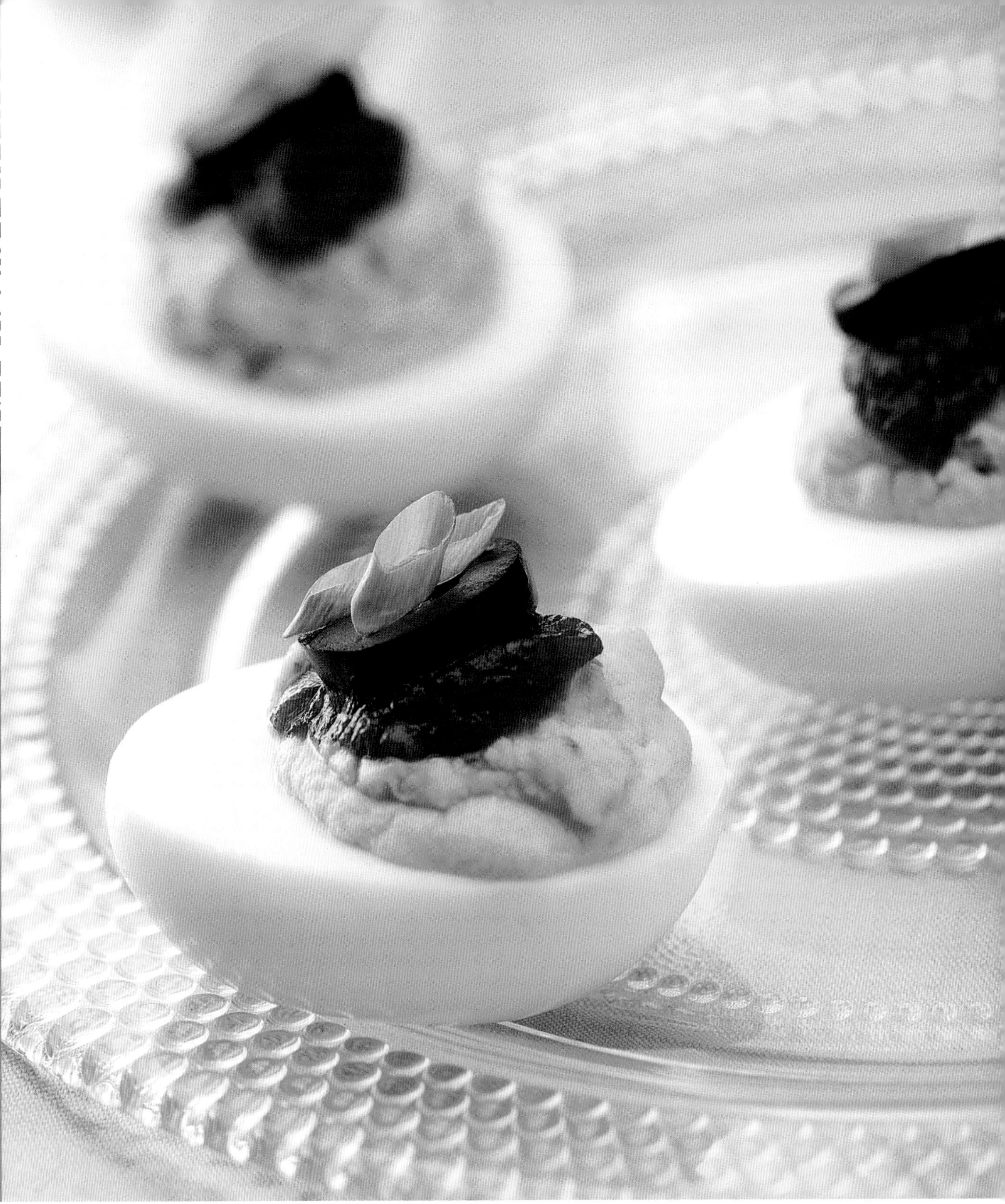

## Santa Fe Deviled Eggs

My deviled eggs have a zippy Southwestern flair. The smoky, spicy flavor is a hit with my husband, Paul.

**—PATRICIA HARMON** BADEN, PA

**START TO FINISH:** 15 MIN.
**MAKES:** 2 SERVINGS

- 2 hard-cooked large eggs
- 1 tablespoon mayonnaise
- 1 tablespoon canned chopped green chilies
- 1/2 teaspoon chipotle pepper in adobo sauce
- 1/8 teaspoon garlic salt
- 4 teaspoons salsa
- 1 1/2 teaspoons thinly sliced green onion
- 1 pitted ripe olive, quartered

**1.** Cut eggs in half lengthwise. Remove yolks; set whites aside. In a small bowl, mash the yolks. Stir in mayonnaise, chilies, chipotle pepper and garlic salt. Stuff or pipe into the egg whites.

**2.** Top with salsa, onion and an olive piece. Refrigerate until serving.

**NUTRITION FACTS** 2 filled egg halves equals 136 cal., 11 g fat (2 g sat. fat), 215 mg chol., 298 mg sodium, 2 g carb. (1 g sugars, 0 fiber), 6 g pro.

**FAST FIX**

## Smoked Turkey Pizza

A chewy pre-baked crust makes quick work of this tasty one-serving pizza. I use out-of-the-ordinary toppings including cranberry sauce and turkey. It's a great way to use up holiday leftovers.

**—LISA VARNER** EL PASO, TX

**START TO FINISH:** 20 MIN.
**MAKES:** 1 SERVING

- 1    pre-baked mini pizza crust
- ¼    cup whole-berry cranberry sauce
- 1    tablespoon chopped onion
- ⅓    cup shredded Monterey Jack cheese
- 2    ounces thinly sliced deli smoked turkey, cut into strips
- 1    teaspoon chopped walnuts

**1.** Place the crust on a baking sheet or pizza pan. Spread with cranberry sauce; sprinkle with onion and cheese. Arrange turkey over cheese; sprinkle with walnuts.

**2.** Bake at 375° for 10-15 minutes or until the cheese is melted.

**NUTRITION FACTS** 1 pizza equals 714 cal., 24 g fat (9 g sat. fat), 55 mg chol., 1551 mg sodium, 93 g carb. (20 g sugars, 3 g fiber), 34 g pro.

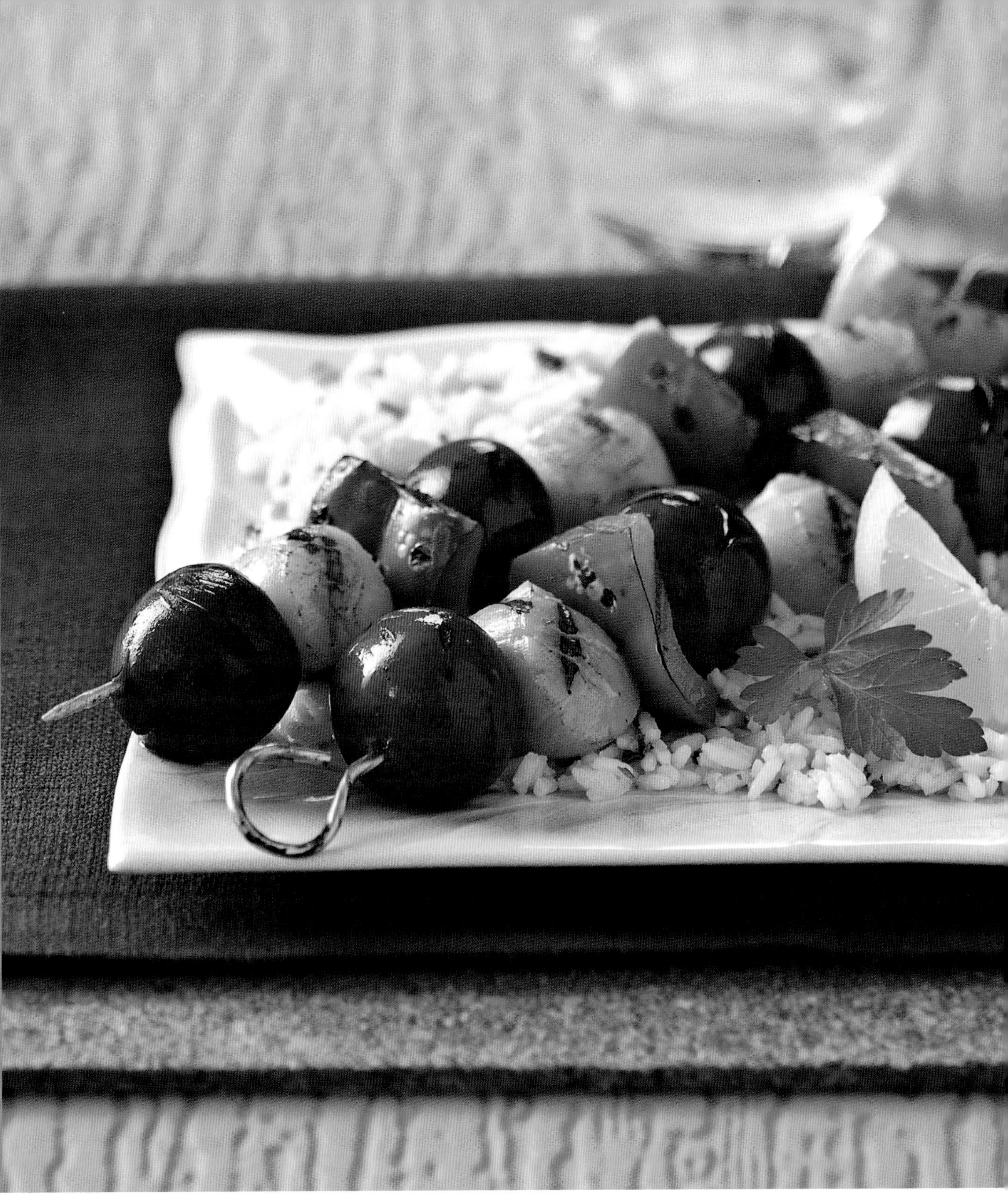

# Scallop Kabobs

I'm always on the lookout for recipes that are lower in fat and heart-healthy, too. These kabobs fill the bill. I like to serve them with a fruit salad and a light dessert.
—**EDIE DESPAIN** LOGAN, UT

**PREP:** 25 MIN. + MARINATING
**GRILL:** 10 MIN.
**MAKES:** 2 SERVINGS

4½ teaspoons lemon juice
4½ teaspoons reduced-sodium
    soy sauce
1   tablespoon canola oil
    Dash garlic powder
    Dash pepper
¾   pound sea scallops
2   small green peppers, cut into
    1½-inch pieces
1   cup cherry tomatoes

**1.** In a small bowl, combine the first five ingredients. Pour 2 tablespoons into a large resealable plastic bag; add scallops. Seal bag and turn to coat; refrigerate for 20 minutes. Cover and refrigerate the remaining marinade to use for basting.

**2.** Meanwhile, in a large saucepan, bring 3 cups water to a boil. Add peppers; cover and boil for 2 minutes. Drain and immediately place peppers in ice water. Drain and pat dry.

**3.** Drain the scallops and discard the marinade. On four metal or soaked wooden skewers, alternately thread the tomatoes, scallops and peppers.

**4.** On a greased grill rack, grill kabobs, covered, over medium heat, or broil 4 in. from the heat for 3-5 minutes on each side or until scallops are firm and opaque, basting occasionally with reserved marinade.

**NUTRITION FACTS** 2 kabobs equals 235 cal., 7 g fat (1 g sat. fat), 56 mg chol., 616 mg sodium, 12 g carb. (4 g sugars, 2 g fiber), 30 g pro. *Diabetic Exchanges:* 4 lean meat, 2 vegetable, 1 fat.

**TOP TIP**

Scallops are commonly found in one of two groups—the sea scallop, yielding 10-20 per pound, or the smaller bay scallop, yielding 60-90 per pound. Scallops are sold fresh or frozen, are usually available shucked, and range in color from pale beige to creamy pink.

APPETIZERS FOR TWO

**FAST FIX** ▶
## Simple Swiss Cheese Fondue
When I was growing up, my friend's mother would make this fondue when I spent the night. Every time I make it, it brings back fond memories. I love the rich flavor. Happy dipping!
—**TRACY LAWSON** FARR WEST, UT

**START TO FINISH:** 20 MIN.
**MAKES:** ⅔ CUP

1    cup (4 ounces) shredded
      Swiss cheese
1    tablespoon all-purpose flour
⅛   teaspoon ground mustard
      Dash ground nutmeg
¼   cup half-and-half cream
¼   cup beer or nonalcoholic beer
4    slices French bread (1 inch thick),
      cut into 1-inch cubes

**1.** In a small bowl, combine cheese, flour, mustard and nutmeg. In a small saucepan, heat cream and beer over medium heat until bubbles form around sides of saucepan. Stir in the cheese mixture. Bring just to a gentle boil; cook and stir for 1-2 minutes or until combined and smooth.

**2.** Transfer to a small fondue pot and keep warm. Serve with bread cubes.

**NUTRITION FACTS** 1 serving equals 395 cal., 19 g fat (12 g sat. fat), 65 mg chol., 433 mg sodium, 30 g carb. (4 g sugars, 1 g fiber), 21 g pro.

**TOP TIP**
Don't like the taste of beer? White wine is a classic ingredient for adding flavor to cheese fondue, so feel free to trade the beer in this recipe for an equal measure of wine. If you're looking for a nonalcoholic option, try vegetable or chicken broth or apple juice, and add a little lemon juice.

# Refreshing Tomato Bruschetta

This recipe is best with sun-warmed tomatoes and basil fresh from the garden. My husband and I love this so much, we can make a meal of it alone.

—**GRETA IGL** MENOMONEE FALLS, WI

**START TO FINISH:** 20 MIN.
**MAKES:** 2 SERVINGS

  3   teaspoons olive oil, divided
  4   slices French bread (1/2 inch thick)
  1   garlic clove, cut in half lengthwise
  3/4   cup chopped seeded tomato
  1   tablespoon minced fresh basil
  1/2   teaspoon minced fresh parsley
  1/2   teaspoon red wine vinegar
  1/8   teaspoon salt
  1/8   teaspoon pepper

**1.** Brush 2 teaspoons oil over one side of each slice of bread; place bread on a baking sheet. Bake at 350° for 5-7 minutes or until lightly browned. Rub cut side of garlic over bread.

**2.** Meanwhile, in a small bowl, combine the tomato, basil, parsley, vinegar, salt, pepper and remaining oil. Spoon onto bread; serve immediately.

**NUTRITION FACTS** 2 slices equals 155 cal., 8 g fat (1 g sat. fat), 0 chol., 327 mg sodium, 19 g carb. (2 g sugars, 2 g fiber), 3 g pro. *Diabetic Exchanges:* 1 1/2 fat, 1 starch.

**(5)INGREDIENTS** **FAST FIX**

# Beef Nachos Supreme

You'll love these beefed-up nachos. They come together in a flash, even when you customize the seasonings and toppings.

**—ROSE LAURITSEN** LINDALE, GA

---

**START TO FINISH:** 25 MIN.
**MAKES:** 2 SERVINGS

---

½   pound lean ground beef (90% lean)
¾   cup water
⅔   cup condensed tomato soup, undiluted
2   tablespoons taco seasoning
¾   cup uncooked instant rice
    Optional toppings: shredded lettuce, shredded cheddar cheese, salsa and sour cream
    Tortilla chips

**1.** In a large skillet, cook beef over medium heat until no longer pink; drain. Stir in water, tomato soup and taco seasoning. Bring to a boil. Stir in rice. Cover and remove from heat. Let stand for 5 minutes or until rice is tender.

**2.** Spoon onto two serving plates. Top as desired. Serve with chips.

**NUTRITION FACTS** 1 serving (calculated without optional toppings and chips) equals 389 cal., 9 g fat (4 g sat. fat), 56 mg chol., 579 mg sodium, 47 g carb. (9 g sugars, 3 g fiber), 27 g pro.

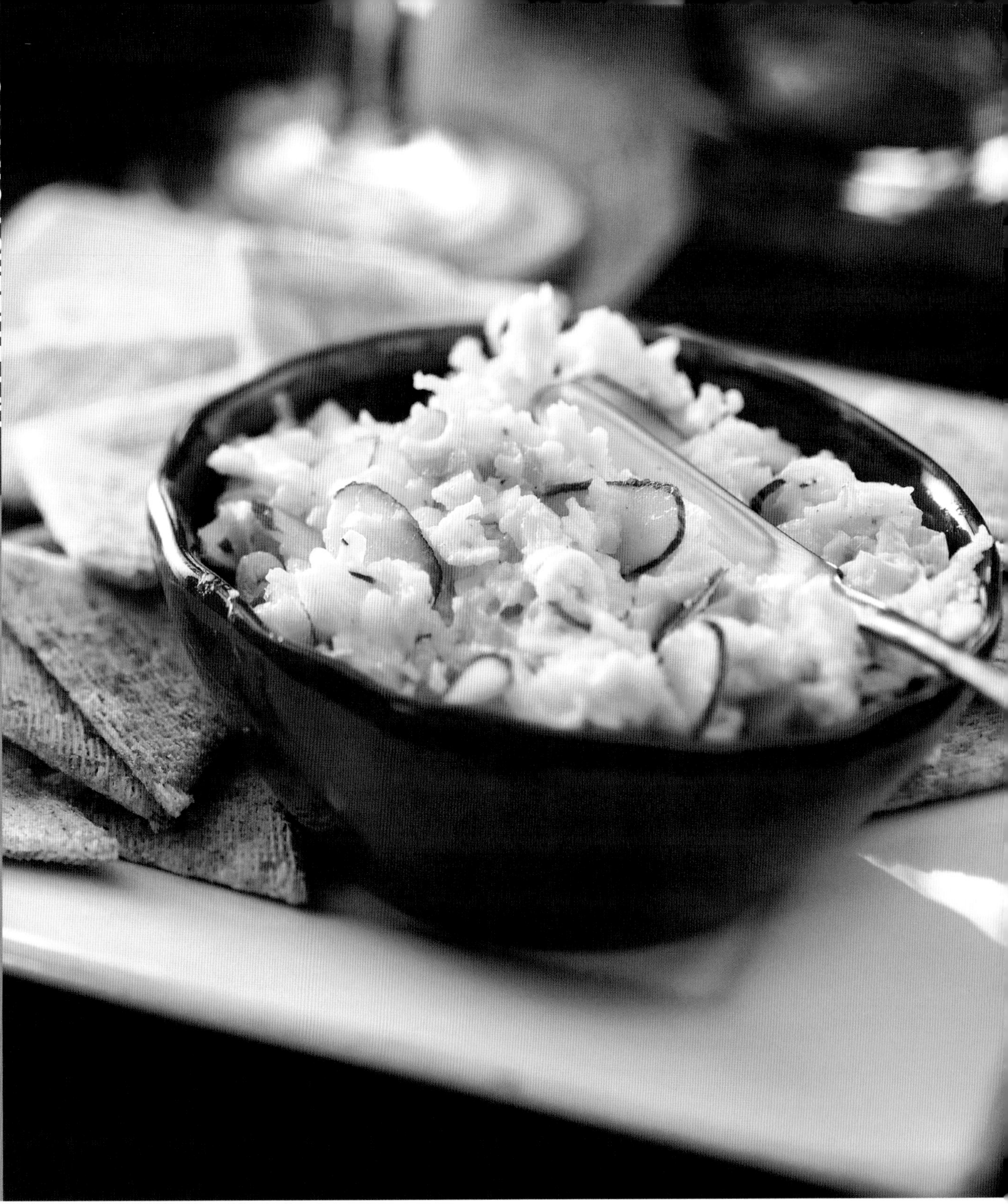

# Almond Cheese Spread

I love this dip recipe! It's a great way to use up different kinds of cheeses I've already got on hand.
—**JOAN COOPER** LAKE ORION, MI

**PREP:** 10 MIN. + CHILLING
**MAKES:** 2 SERVINGS

½ cup shredded sharp white cheddar cheese
2 tablespoons mayonnaise
⅛ teaspoon onion powder
   Dash pepper
   Dash Louisiana-style hot sauce
1 green onion, chopped
1 tablespoon sliced almonds
   Celery ribs or assorted crackers

In a small bowl, combine the first five ingredients; stir in green onion and almonds. Cover and refrigerate for at least 4 hours. Serve with celery or crackers.

**NUTRITION FACTS** ¼ cup (calculated without celery and crackers) equals 185 cal., 16 g fat (7 g sat. fat), 35 mg chol., 297 mg sodium, 3 g carb. (1 g sugars, 1 g fiber), 8 g pro.

**TOP TIP**

Toasting nuts deepens their flavor and gives them added crunch. To toast almonds, place them on a baking sheet and heat in a 325° oven for 5-7 minutes, stirring once or twice. Alternatively, cook them in a large skillet over medium heat, tossing regularly. For a variation, try ground or finely chopped almonds instead of sliced.

EAT SMART FAST FIX

# Herbed Tortilla Chips

I came up with these when I found several packages of tortilla shells while cleaning out my freezer. It's an inexpensive, low-calorie treat for my husband and me.

**—ANGELA CASE** MONTICELLO, AR

**START TO FINISH:** 20 MIN.
**MAKES:** 3 SERVINGS

- 2 teaspoons grated Parmesan cheese
- 1/2 teaspoon dried oregano
- 1/2 teaspoon dried parsley flakes
- 1/2 teaspoon dried rosemary, crushed
- 1/4 teaspoon garlic powder
- 1/8 teaspoon kosher salt
  Dash pepper
- 2 flour tortillas (6 inches)
- 2 teaspoons olive oil

**1.** In a small bowl, combine the first seven ingredients. Brush tortillas with oil; cut each tortilla into six wedges. Arrange in a single layer on a baking sheet coated with cooking spray.

**2.** Sprinkle wedges with seasoning mixture. Bake at 425° for 5-7 minutes or until golden brown. Cool for 5 minutes.

**NUTRITION FACTS** 4 chips equals 94 cal., 5 g fat (1 g sat. fat), 1 mg chol., 245 mg sodium, 9 g carb. (0 sugars, 0 fiber), 3 g pro. *Diabetic Exchanges:* 1 fat, 1/2 starch.

# Deep-Fried Onions with Dipping Sauce

Enjoy this steak house appetizer right in your own home. Our Test Kitchen covered onion wedges with a golden batter and fried them to perfection. The spicy dipping sauce really heats things up!

**—*TASTE OF HOME* TEST KITCHEN**

**START TO FINISH:** 25 MIN.
**MAKES:** 2 SERVINGS

| | |
|---|---|
| 1 | sweet onion |
| ½ | cup all-purpose flour |
| 1 | teaspoon paprika |
| ½ | teaspoon garlic powder |
| ⅛ | teaspoon cayenne pepper |
| ⅛ | teaspoon pepper |

**BEER BATTER**

| | |
|---|---|
| ⅓ | cup all-purpose flour |
| 1 | tablespoon cornstarch |
| ½ | teaspoon garlic powder |
| ½ | teaspoon paprika |
| ¼ | teaspoon salt |
| ¼ | teaspoon pepper |
| 7 | tablespoons beer or nonalcoholic beer |
| | Oil for deep-fat frying |

**DIPPING SAUCE**

| | |
|---|---|
| ¼ | cup sour cream |
| 2 | tablespoons chili sauce |
| ¼ | teaspoon ground cumin |
| ⅛ | teaspoon cayenne pepper |

**1.** Cut onion into 1-in. wedges and separate into pieces. In a shallow bowl, combine flour, paprika, garlic powder, cayenne and pepper.

**2.** For the batter, in another shallow bowl, combine the flour, cornstarch, garlic powder, paprika, salt and pepper. Stir in beer. Dip the onion wedges in the dry flour mixture, then in the batter and again in the dry flour mixture.

**3.** In an electric skillet or deep-fat fryer, heat oil to 375°. Fry the onion wedges, a few at a time, for 1-2 minutes on each side or until golden brown. Drain on paper towels. In a small bowl, combine the sauce ingredients. Serve with onions.

**NUTRITION FACTS** 1 serving equals 686 cal., 12 g fat (7 g sat. fat), 40 mg chol., 1085 mg sodium, 119 g carb. (20 g sugars, 7 g fiber), 16 g pro.

EAT SMART **FAST FIX**

## Easy Mango Salsa

This recipe puts a tantalizing twist on salsa. Tangy fruit, savory onion and peppy hot sauce work in perfect harmony to create a fun appetizer that's good for you, too!

**—KRISTINE SIMS** ST JOSEPH, MI

**START TO FINISH:** 15 MIN.
**MAKES:** 1 1/2 CUPS

- ½ cup finely chopped tart apple
- ½ cup finely chopped peeled mango
- ½ cup canned crushed pineapple
- 2 green onions, thinly sliced
- 2 tablespoons minced fresh cilantro
- 3 to 5 drops hot pepper sauce, optional
  Tortilla chips

In a small bowl, combine the apple, mango, pineapple, onions, cilantro and, if desired, pepper sauce. Chill until serving. Serve with tortilla chips.

**NUTRITION FACTS** ½ cup equals 62 cal., 0 fat (0 sat. fat), 0 chol., 3 mg sodium, 16 g carb. (14 g sugars, 2 g fiber), 1 g pro. *Diabetic Exchanges:* ½ starch, ½ fruit.

APPETIZERS FOR TWO

# Crab Cakes with Lime Sauce

Reel in a breezy taste of the seashore with these delectable, nicely coated crab cakes. The lip-smacking lime sauce adds a refreshing, summery tang.
—**MARJIE GASPAR** OXFORD, PA

**START TO FINISH:** 25 MIN.
**MAKES:** 3 SERVINGS

- 2 cans (6 ounces each) lump crabmeat, drained
- 1 green onion, chopped
- 1 tablespoon Dijon mustard
- 1 teaspoon Italian salad dressing mix
- 1½ cups crushed butter-flavored crackers (about 35), divided
- 1 cup mayonnaise, divided
- 2 tablespoons lime juice, divided
- ¼ cup canola oil
- ¼ cup sour cream
- 1½ teaspoons grated lime peel

**1.** In a large bowl, combine the crab, onion, mustard, dressing mix, 1 cup cracker crumbs, ½ cup mayonnaise and 1 tablespoon lime juice. Shape into six patties; coat with the remaining cracker crumbs.

**2.** In a large skillet, heat oil over medium heat. Cook the crab cakes for 3-4 minutes on each side or until lightly browned.

**3.** For the lime sauce, in a small bowl, combine the sour cream, lime peel, and the remaining mayonnaise and lime juice until blended. Serve with the crab cakes.

**NUTRITION FACTS** 2 crab cakes with ¼ cup dip equals 1039 cal., 92 g fat (15 g sat. fat), 90 mg chol., 1207 mg sodium, 34 g carb. (5 g sugars, 1 g fiber), 16 g pro.

**Autumn Chowder, p. 82**

# Soups for Two

Soups make for classic menus all year long. If you're not a fan of leftovers, however, why not scale down and make a delicious soup that serves just two?

**Best Chicken Tortilla Soup, p. 74**

**Mexican Shrimp Bisque, p. 66**

**Curry Chicken Soup, p. 81**

FAST FIX ▶

# Lemon-Chicken Velvet Soup

Here's the perfect antidote to a chilly spring day. The lively flavor of lemon perks up a rich chicken soup accented with sugar snap peas.

**—CELESTE BUCKLEY** REDDING, CA

**START TO FINISH:** 25 MIN.
**MAKES:** 2 SERVINGS

- 2 tablespoons butter
- 2 tablespoons all-purpose flour
- 1 can (14½ ounces) chicken broth
- 3 tablespoons lemon juice
- 1½ cups cubed cooked chicken breast
- 10 fresh or frozen sugar snap peas
- 2 tablespoons minced fresh parsley
- 1 teaspoon grated lemon peel
- 3 tablespoons heavy whipping cream

**1.** In a small saucepan, melt butter. Stir in flour until smooth; gradually add broth and lemon juice. Bring to a boil; cook and stir for 1-2 minutes or until thickened.

**2.** Stir in chicken, peas, parsley and lemon peel; cook 2-3 minutes longer or until the chicken is heated through and the peas are crisp-tender. Stir in cream; heat through (do not boil).

**NUTRITION FACTS** 1¼ cups equals 352 cal., 18 g fat (10 g sat. fat), 131 mg chol., 730 mg sodium, 13 g carb. (4 g sugars, 2 g fiber), 37 g pro.

# Hearty Sausage Chili

You'll have a stick-to-the-ribs bowl of chili in no time—it doesn't need to cook for hours! This chili goes well with corn bread.

**—JEANNIE KLUGH** LANCASTER, PA

---

**PREP:** 10 MIN. • **COOK:** 25 MIN.
**MAKES:** 3 SERVINGS

---

| | |
|---|---|
| ½ | pound bulk Italian sausage |
| 1 | small sweet yellow pepper, diced |
| 1 | small sweet red pepper, diced |
| 1 | teaspoon canola oil |
| 1 | to 2 garlic cloves, minced |
| 1 | can (15 ounces) crushed tomatoes |
| ¾ | cup hot chili beans |
| 2 | tablespoons chili sauce |
| 2 | teaspoons chili powder |
| 1 | teaspoon ground cumin |
| | Sour cream, optional |

**1.** In a large saucepan, saute sausage and peppers in oil until meat is no longer pink. Add garlic; cook 1 minute longer. Drain.

**2.** Stir in tomatoes, beans, chili sauce, chili powder and cumin. Bring to a boil. Reduce heat; simmer, uncovered, for 20 minutes or until heated through. Serve with sour cream if desired.

**NUTRITION FACTS** 1⅓ cups equals 256 cal., 10 g fat (2 g sat. fat), 45 mg chol., 1051 mg sodium, 26 g carb. (3 g sugars, 7 g fiber), 18 g pro.

FAST FIX ▶

## Mexican Shrimp Bisque

I enjoy both Cajun and Mexican cuisine, and this rich, elegant soup combines the best of both. I serve it with a crispy green salad and glass of white wine for a simple but special meal.

**—KAREN HARRIS** CASTLE PINES, CO

**START TO FINISH:** 30 MIN.
**MAKES:** 3 SERVINGS

| | |
|---|---|
| 1 | small onion, chopped |
| 1 | tablespoon olive oil |
| 2 | garlic cloves, minced |
| 1 | tablespoon all-purpose flour |
| 1 | cup water |
| ½ | cup heavy whipping cream |
| 2 | teaspoons chicken bouillon granules |
| 1 | tablespoon chili powder |
| ½ | teaspoon ground cumin |
| ½ | teaspoon ground coriander |
| ½ | pound uncooked medium shrimp, peeled and deveined |
| ½ | cup sour cream |
| | Chopped fresh cilantro and sliced avocado, optional |

**1.** In a small saucepan, saute onion in oil until tender. Add garlic; cook 1 minute longer. Stir in flour until blended. Stir in water, cream, bouillon and seasonings; bring to a boil. Reduce heat; cover and simmer for 5 minutes.

**2.** Cut shrimp into bite-size pieces if desired; add shrimp to soup. Simmer 5-10 minutes longer or until the shrimp turn pink. Place sour cream in a small bowl; gradually stir in ½ cup hot soup. Return all to the pan, stirring constantly. Heat through (do not boil). Top with cilantro and avocado if desired.

**NUTRITION FACTS** 1 cup equals 357 cal., 28 g fat (15 g sat. fat), 173 mg chol., 706 mg sodium, 10 g carb. (3 g sugars, 2 g fiber), 16 g pro.

# Homemade Lentil Barley Stew

Green chilies and fresh ginger add zip to this thick meatless stew. It can be served as is or with a dollop of sour cream on top.
—**ERIN MONROE** OVIEDO, FL

**PREP:** 10 MIN. • **COOK:** 50 MIN.
**MAKES:** 2 SERVINGS

| | |
|---|---|
| 1 | medium carrot, chopped |
| 1 | small onion, chopped |
| 1 | celery rib, chopped |
| 1 | teaspoon minced fresh gingerroot |
| 2 | teaspoons olive oil |
| 1 | garlic clove, minced |
| 1/4 | cup dried lentils, rinsed |
| 1/4 | cup medium pearl barley |
| 1 | can (10 ounces) diced tomatoes with mild green chilies |
| 1 | cup water |
| 1 | cup vegetable broth |
| 1/4 | teaspoon ground cumin |
| 1 | tablespoon reduced-sodium soy sauce |

1. In a large saucepan, saute the carrot, onion, celery and ginger in olive oil until crisp-tender. Add garlic; cook 1 minute longer. Add lentils and barley; cook for 3 minutes, stirring occasionally.

2. Stir in tomatoes, water, broth and cumin. Bring to a boil. Reduce heat; cover and simmer for 20 minutes, stirring occasionally. Add soy sauce; simmer 20-30 minutes longer or until the lentils and barley are tender.

**NUTRITION FACTS** 1½ cups equals 304 cal., 5 g fat (1 g sat. fat), 0 chol., 1356 mg sodium, 54 g carb. (13 g sugars, 15 g fiber), 11 g pro.

**DID YOU KNOW?**

Unlike dried beans, lentils don't have to be soaked before using. They are a quick-to-cook source of iron, most B vitamins and fiber. Cup for cup, lentils have twice as much protein and iron as quinoa.

EAT SMART **FAST FIX**

## Creamy Spring Soup

At the end of a long day, there's not much better than indulging in a bowl of this warm, creamy soup. It comes together in a flash, and with so many fresh, delicious veggies, you know you're filling up on nutrition, too.

**—DORA HANDY** ALLIANCE, OH

**START TO FINISH:** 25 MIN.
**MAKES:** 2 SERVINGS

- 1   can (14½ ounces) reduced-sodium chicken broth
- 4   fresh asparagus spears, trimmed and cut into 2-inch pieces
- 4   baby carrots, julienned
- ½   celery rib, chopped
- 1   green onion, chopped
      Dash garlic powder
      Dash pepper
- ¾   cup cooked elbow macaroni
- 1   can (5½ ounces) evaporated milk
- ¾   cup fresh baby spinach

In a large saucepan, combine the first seven ingredients. Bring to a boil. Reduce heat; cover and simmer for 5 minutes or until the vegetables are tender. Stir in macaroni, milk and spinach; heat through.

**NUTRITION FACTS** 1⅓ cup equals 207 cal., 6 g fat (4 g sat. fat), 28 mg chol., 677 mg sodium, 26 g carb. (12 g sugars, 2 g fiber), 12 g pro. *Diabetic Exchanges:* 1 starch, 1 vegetable, ½ whole milk.

# Veggie Salmon Chowder

I wanted to use up odds and ends in my fridge (waste not, want not!) and came up with this chowder. It began as an experiment but has become a mainstay.
—**LIV VORS** PETERBOROUGH, ON

**START TO FINISH:** 30 MIN.
**MAKES:** 2 SERVINGS

|   |   |
|---|---|
| 1 | medium sweet potato, peeled and cut into 1/2-inch cubes |
| 1 | cup reduced-sodium chicken broth |
| 1/2 | cup fresh or frozen corn |
| 1/2 | small onion, chopped |
| 2 | garlic cloves, minced |
| 1 1/2 | cups fresh spinach, torn |
| 1/2 | cup flaked smoked salmon fillet |
| 1 | teaspoon pickled jalapeno slices, chopped |
| 1 | tablespoon cornstarch |
| 1/2 | cup 2% milk |
| 1 | tablespoon minced fresh cilantro Dash pepper |

**1.** In a large saucepan, combine the first five ingredients; bring to a boil. Reduce heat; simmer, covered, 8-10 minutes or until the potato is tender.

**2.** Stir in spinach, salmon and jalapeno; cook 1-2 minutes or until the spinach is wilted. In a small bowl, mix cornstarch and milk until smooth; stir into the soup. Bring to a boil; cook and stir 2 minutes or until thickened. Stir in cilantro and pepper.

**NUTRITION FACTS** 1 1/4 cups equals 202 cal., 3 g fat (1 g sat. fat), 12 mg chol., 645 mg sodium, 32 g carb. (11 g sugars, 4 g fiber), 13 g pro. *Diabetic Exchanges:* 2 starch, 1 lean meat, 1 vegetable.

# Best Chicken Tortilla Soup

This rich soup is perfect for using up garden-fresh bounty.

—**KATHY AVERBECK** DOUSMAN, WI

**PREP:** 30 MIN. • **COOK:** 25 MIN.
**MAKES:** 3½ CUPS

- 2 medium tomatoes
- 1 small onion, cut into wedges
- 1 garlic clove, peeled
- 4 teaspoons canola oil, divided
- 1 boneless skinless chicken breast half (6 ounces)
- ¼ teaspoon lemon-pepper seasoning
- ⅛ teaspoon salt
- 2 corn tortillas (6 inches)
- ½ cup diced zucchini
- 2 tablespoons chopped carrot
- 1 tablespoon minced fresh cilantro
- ¾ teaspoon ground cumin
- ½ teaspoon chili powder
- 1 cup reduced-sodium chicken broth
- ½ cup Spicy Hot V8 juice
- ⅓ cup frozen corn
- 2 tablespoons tomato puree
- 1½ teaspoons chopped and seeded jalapeno pepper
- 1 bay leaf
- ¼ cup cubed or sliced avocado
- ¼ cup shredded Mexican cheese blend

**1.** Brush tomatoes, onion and garlic with 1 teaspoon oil. Broil 4 in. from the heat for 6-8 minutes or until tender, turning once. Peel and discard charred tomato skins; place tomatoes in a blender. Add onion and garlic; cover and process for 1-2 minutes or until smooth.

**2.** Sprinkle chicken with lemon pepper and salt; broil for 5-6 minutes on each side or until a thermometer reads 170°. Cut one tortilla into ¼-in. strips; coarsely chop the remaining tortilla.

**3.** In a large saucepan, heat the remaining oil. Fry the tortilla strips until crisp and browned; remove with a slotted spoon.

**4.** In the same pan, cook zucchini, carrot, cilantro, cumin, chili powder and chopped tortilla over medium heat for 4 minutes. Stir in the tomato mixture, broth, V8 juice, corn, tomato puree, jalapeno and bay leaf. Bring to a boil. Reduce heat; simmer, uncovered, for 20 minutes.

**5.** Cut chicken into strips and add to soup; heat through. Discard the bay leaf. Garnish with avocado, cheese and the tortilla strips.

**NOTE** Wear disposable gloves when cutting hot peppers; the oils can burn skin. Avoid touching your face.

**NUTRITION FACTS** 1¼ cups equals 284 cal., 14 g fat (3 g sat. fat), 40 mg chol., 617 mg sodium, 24 g carb. (7 g sugars, 5 g fiber), 18 g pro.

# Italian Sausage Minestrone

Come in from the cold with this no-fuss minestrone. Feeling daring? Substitute a can of butter beans or pinto beans for one of the cans of cannellini beans.

**—ELIZABETH RENTERIA** VANCOUVER, WA

**PREP:** 20 MIN. + FREEZING
**COOK:** 1¼ HOURS
**MAKES:** 3 SERVINGS

- ¼ pound bulk Italian sausage
- ⅓ cup chopped carrot
- ¼ cup chopped celery
- 3 tablespoons chopped onion
- 1 garlic cloves, minced
- 2¼ teaspoons olive oil
- 1¾ cups reduced-sodium chicken broth
- ¾ cup cannellini beans, rinsed and drained
- ¾ cup undrained fire-roasted diced tomatoes
- 1 bay leaf
- ¾ teaspoon Italian seasoning
- ¾ teaspoon tomato paste
- ¼ cup ditalini or other small pasta
  Shredded or shaved Parmesan cheese

**1.** In a Dutch oven, cook sausage over medium heat until no longer pink; drain.

**2.** In the same pot, saute carrot, celery, onion and garlic in oil until tender. Stir in broth, beans, tomatoes, bay leaf, Italian seasoning, tomato paste and sausage. Bring to a boil. Reduce heat; cover and simmer for 30 minutes.

**3.** Stir in ditalini and return to a boil. Reduce heat and cook, uncovered, for 6-8 minutes or until the pasta is tender. Discard bay leaf. Serve with cheese.

**NUTRITION FACTS** 1 serving equals 296 cal., 16 g fat (5 g sat. fat), 29 mg chol., 875 mg sodium, 26 g carb. (4 g sugars, 4 g fiber), 12 g pro.

**FAST FIX** ▶

## Quick Broccoli Cheese Soup

Frozen broccoli-cheese sauce makes this hearty soup a speedy addition to a lunchtime or evening meal. It's also a tasty way to use up leftover rice, and the recipe can easily be doubled, too.
**—LAURA MIHALENKO-DEVOE** CHARLOTTE, NC

**START TO FINISH:** 25 MIN.
**MAKES:** 2 SERVINGS

- 2 tablespoons chopped onion
- 1 tablespoon butter
- 1 cup chicken broth
- 1 package (10 ounces) frozen broccoli with cheese sauce, thawed
- ½ cup cooked long grain rice
- ¼ cup heavy whipping cream

**1.** In a small saucepan, cook onion in butter until tender. Stir in broth and broccoli with sauce. Bring to a boil. Reduce heat; simmer, uncovered, for 4 minutes.

**2.** Add rice and cream. Cook 3-4 minutes longer or until heated through and the broccoli is tender (do not boil).

**NUTRITION FACTS** 1¼ cups equals 268 cal., 18 g fat (11 g sat. fat), 51 mg chol., 829 mg sodium, 21 g carb. (6 g sugars, 2 g fiber), 9 g pro.

## Curry Chicken Soup

Don't be overwhelmed by the ingredient list—this soup is quick and easy to make. Plus, it's a fantastic way to get your veggies!

—**JANE HACKER** MILWAUKEE, WI

---

**PREP:** 20 MIN. • **COOK:** 15 MIN.
**MAKES:** 2 SERVINGS

---

- ¼ pound boneless skinless chicken breasts, cut into ½-inch cubes
- 1½ teaspoons canola oil, divided
- ⅓ cup chopped onion
- ¼ cup chopped carrot
- ¼ cup chopped celery
- ¼ cup chopped green pepper
- ½ cup chopped peeled apple
- 1 tablespoon all-purpose flour
- ⅛ teaspoon salt
- 1 can (14½ ounces) reduced-sodium chicken broth
- 2 tablespoons tomato paste
- 1 to 1½ teaspoons curry powder
- ½ teaspoon ground ginger
- ⅛ to ¼ teaspoon crushed red pepper flakes
- 1 tablespoon minced fresh parsley

**1.** In a large saucepan coated with cooking spray, cook chicken in ½ teaspoon oil for 4-5 minutes or until the juices run clear. Remove chicken and set it aside.

**2.** In the same saucepan, saute onion, carrot, celery and green pepper in the remaining oil for 4 minutes. Add apple; cook 2 minutes longer. Combine flour and salt. Sprinkle over the vegetable mixture; cook and stir for 1 minute. Gradually stir in broth and tomato paste. Bring to a boil; cook and stir 1-2 minutes longer or until slightly thickened.

**3.** Stir in the curry, ginger and pepper flakes. Return the chicken to saucepan and bring to a boil. Reduce heat; simmer, uncovered, for 8-10 minutes or until the vegetables are tender. Sprinkle with the minced parsley.

**NUTRITION FACTS** 1½ cups equals 177 cal., 5 g fat (1 g sat. fat), 31 mg chol., 728 mg sodium, 17 g carb. (8 g sugars, 3 g fiber), 17 g pro. *Diabetic Exchanges:* 2 lean meat, 2 vegetable, ½ starch, ½ fat.

## Autumn Chowder

When the weather gets chilly, we enjoy comfort foods like this hearty chowder. It's easy to prepare, and the aroma of it as it simmers will make mouths water.

—**SHEENA HOFFMAN** NORTH VANCOUVER, BC

**PREP:** 10 MIN. • **COOK:** 35 MIN.
**MAKES:** 2 SERVINGS

| | |
|---|---|
| 2 | bacon strips, diced |
| 1/4 | cup chopped onion |
| 1 | medium red potato, cubed |
| 1 | small carrot, halved lengthwise and thinly sliced |
| 1/2 | cup water |
| 3/4 | teaspoon chicken bouillon granules |
| 1 | cup milk |
| 2/3 | cup frozen corn |
| 1/8 | teaspoon pepper |
| 2 1/2 | teaspoons all-purpose flour |
| 2 | tablespoons cold water |
| 3/4 | cup shredded cheddar cheese |

**1.** In a large saucepan, cook bacon over medium heat until crisp; remove to paper towels. Drain pan, reserving 1 teaspoon drippings. In the drippings, saute onion until tender. Add potato, carrot, water and bouillon. Bring to a boil. Reduce heat; cover and simmer for 15-20 minutes or until the vegetables are almost tender.

**2.** Stir in milk, corn and pepper. Cook 5 minutes longer. Combine flour and cold water until smooth; gradually whisk into the soup. Bring to a boil; cook and stir for 1-2 minutes or until thickened. Remove from the heat; stir in cheese until melted. Sprinkle with the bacon.

**NUTRITION FACTS** 1 cup equals 473 cal., 30 g fat (16 g sat. fat), 77 mg chol., 810 mg sodium, 35 g carb. (10 g sugars, 4 g fiber), 19 g pro.

## Bart's Black Bean Soup

Every cook can appreciate a fresh, simple soup that's ready in minutes. Add a salad and dinner rolls or quesadillas for a complete meal that hits the spot.

**—SHARON ULLYOT** LONDON, ON

**START TO FINISH:** 10 MIN.
**MAKES:** 2 SERVINGS

| | |
|---|---|
| ¾ | cup canned black beans, rinsed and drained |
| ¾ | cup chicken broth |
| ⅓ | cup salsa |
| ¼ | cup whole kernel corn |
| | Dash hot pepper sauce |
| 1 | teaspoon lime juice |
| ½ | cup shredded cheddar cheese |
| 1 | tablespoon chopped green onion |

In a microwave-safe bowl, combine the first five ingredients. Cover and microwave on high for 2 minutes or until heated through. Pour into two serving bowls; drizzle each with lime juice. Sprinkle with cheese and green onions.

**NOTE** This recipe was tested in a 1,100-watt microwave.

**NUTRITION FACTS** 1 cup equals 218 cal., 8 g fat (6 g sat. fat), 32 mg chol., 964 mg sodium, 22 g carb. (4 g sugars, 4 g fiber), 11 g pro.

EAT SMART

## Roasted Tomato Soup with Fresh Basil

Here's a tasty way to use up garden tomatoes. The thyme and basil make this soup taste much fresher than canned varieties.
—**MARIE FORTE** RARITAN, NJ

**PREP:** 40 MIN. • **COOK:** 5 MIN.
**MAKES:** 2 SERVINGS

1¼ pounds tomatoes (about 4 medium), halved
1 small onion, quartered
1 garlic clove, peeled and halved
1 tablespoon olive oil
1 tablespoon minced fresh thyme
½ teaspoon salt
⅛ teaspoon pepper
4 fresh basil leaves
   Salad croutons and additional fresh basil leaves, optional

**1.** Place the tomatoes, onion and garlic in a greased 15x10x1-in. baking pan; drizzle with oil. Sprinkle with thyme, salt and pepper; toss to coat. Bake at 400° for 25-30 minutes or until tender, stirring once. Cool slightly.

**2.** In a blender, process the tomato mixture and basil leaves until blended. Transfer to a large saucepan and heat through. If desired, garnish each serving with croutons and additional basil.

**NUTRITION FACTS** 1 cup equals 129 cal., 7 g fat (1 g sat. fat), 0 chol., 606 mg sodium, 15 g carb. (9 g sugars, 4 g fiber), 3 g pro. *Diabetic Exchanges:* 3 vegetable, 1 fat.

**Pork Burgers with Grilled Pineapple & Peppers, p. 98**

# Sandwiches for Two

Paired with soup, served with salad or enjoyed all on their own, these sandwiches, burgers and wraps are great for lunch, dinner or even brunch!

**Chicken Gyros, p. 109**

**Wonderburgers, p. 105**

**Bacon, Egg & Avocado Sandwiches, p. 90**

**FAST FIX** ▶

# Bacon, Egg & Avocado Sandwiches

My husband wanted bacon and eggs, while I wanted a BLT. We settled our standoff with an irresistible sandwich we've had many times since.

—**PATTI DARWIN** LUBBOCK, TX

---

**START TO FINISH:** 25 MIN.
**MAKES:** 2 SERVINGS

---

- 2   bacon strips, halved crosswise
- 2   large eggs
- 1/8   teaspoon garlic salt
- 1/8   teaspoon pepper
- 2   tablespoons mayonnaise
- 4   slices sourdough bread, toasted
- 4   thin slices tomato
- 1/2   medium ripe avocado, peeled and sliced
- 2   slices Gouda cheese, optional
- 1   slice red onion, separated into rings, optional
- 2   teaspoons butter, softened

**1.** In a large nonstick skillet, cook bacon over medium heat until crisp. Remove to paper towels to drain. Pour off drippings.

**2.** Break the eggs, one at a time, into the same skillet; immediately reduce the heat to low. Cook until the whites are completely set and the yolks begin to thicken. Remove from heat; sprinkle with garlic salt and pepper.

**3.** Spread mayonnaise over two slices of toast. Top with the bacon, eggs, tomato, avocado and, if desired, cheese and onion. Spread butter over the remaining toast; place over top.

**NOTE** Avocados are known for their healthy monounsaturated fat, but they are also a good source of vitamins C, K and E plus most B vitamins.

**NUTRITION FACTS** 1 sandwich equals 448 cal., 23 g fat (7 g sat. fat), 209 mg chol., 864 mg sodium, 44 g carb. (7 g sugars, 4 g fiber), 18 g pro.

# Smoked Salmon Bagel Sandwiches

A memorable pesto salmon I tried in Hawaii inspired these super convenient sandwiches. Pack them in a lunch, or serve them on a brunch buffet.

**—SHERRYL VERA** HURLBURT FIELD, FL

---

**START TO FINISH:** 10 MIN.
**MAKES:** 2 SERVINGS

---

- 2 tablespoons prepared pesto
- 2 whole wheat bagels, split and toasted
- 1/8 teaspoon coarsely ground pepper
- 4 to 5 ounces smoked salmon or lox
- 2 slices tomato
- 2 Bibb or Boston lettuce leaves

Spread pesto over bagel bottoms; sprinkle with pepper. Layer with salmon, tomato and lettuce leaves. Replace tops.

**NUTRITION FACTS** 1 sandwich equals 295 cal., 10 g fat (3 g sat. fat), 18 mg chol., 1551 mg sodium, 33 g carb. (2 g sugars, 6 g fiber), 19 g pro.

**TOP TIP**

Now that you've discovered this delicious flavor combination, try it in other ways. Smear pesto on crackers or slices of French baguette and top with a curl of smoked salmon for an appetizer. Or, if you're in the mood for a hot breakfast, add small chunks of smoked salmon to scrambled eggs, along with pesto or finely chopped fresh basil.

**FAST FIX**

# Avocado Turkey Wraps

These delicious sandwiches are perfect for brown-bag lunches. With layers of sliced turkey, avocado and cheese, they'll add extra flavor to noontime meals.

*—TASTE OF HOME* **TEST KITCHEN**

**START TO FINISH:** 15 MIN.
**MAKES:** 2 SERVINGS

- 2 whole wheat tortillas (8 inches), room temperature
- 2 tablespoons fat-free mayonnaise
- ¼ pound thinly sliced deli turkey
- 8 thin slices tomato
- 2 teaspoons finely chopped jalapeno pepper
- ¼ cup shredded reduced-fat cheddar cheese
- 2 teaspoons minced fresh cilantro
- ½ medium ripe avocado, peeled and thinly sliced

Spread tortillas with mayonnaise. Top each with turkey, tomato, jalapeno, cheese, cilantro and avocado. Roll up and cut in half.

**NOTE** Wear disposable gloves when cutting hot peppers; the oils can burn skin. Avoid touching your face.

**NUTRITION FACTS** 1 wrap equals 342 cal., 15 g fat (4 g sat. fat), 37 mg chol., 1079 mg sodium, 34 g carb. (5 g sugars, 6 g fiber), 18 g pro.

# Spicy Chicken Tomato Pitas

This is a terrific recipe, nice and light. It cooks up quickly, too, which is always a big bonus. A sizzling blend of Southwest tastes with a bright splash of lemon in an easy-to-eat pita shell, this one's a crowd pleaser!

**—CORI COOPER** BOISE, ID

---

**START TO FINISH:** 30 MIN.
**MAKES:** 2 SERVINGS

### TOMATO RELISH
- 2 medium tomatoes, seeded and chopped
- 1/4 cup chopped onion
- 2 tablespoons minced fresh parsley
- 2 tablespoons lemon juice
- 1 1/2 teaspoons olive oil
- 1/2 teaspoon ground coriander
- 1/2 teaspoon ground cumin
- 1/8 teaspoon crushed red pepper flakes

### CHICKEN PITAS
- 1 1/2 teaspoons ground cumin
- 1 1/2 teaspoons paprika
- 3/4 teaspoon dried oregano
- 3/4 teaspoon ground coriander
- 1/4 teaspoon crushed red pepper flakes
- 1/8 teaspoon salt
- 2 boneless skinless chicken breast halves (4 ounces each)
- 4 whole wheat pita pocket halves

**1.** Combine the relish ingredients; chill until serving.

**2.** Combine cumin, paprika, oregano, coriander, pepper flakes and salt; rub over both sides of chicken. Grill the chicken, covered, over medium heat or broil 4 in. from the heat for 4-7 minutes on each side or until juices run clear.

**3.** Slice the chicken. Fill each pita half with chicken and tomato relish.

**NUTRITION FACTS** 2 pita halves equals 362 cal., 9 g fat (2 g sat. fat), 63 mg chol., 516 mg sodium, 43 g carb. (6 g sugars, 9 g fiber), 31 g pro. *Diabetic Exchanges:* 3 lean meat, 2 starch, 1 vegetable, 1 fat.

**FAST FIX**

# Pork Burgers with Grilled Pineapple & Peppers

I had ground pork and fresh pineapple on hand, so I made these burgers. My hubby loves them in grilling season—we serve them with slaw and roasted potato wedges.
—**HOPE WASYLENKI** GAHANNA, OH

**START TO FINISH:** 30 MIN.
**MAKES:** 2 SERVINGS

- 3 tablespoons Dijon mustard
- 2 tablespoons honey
- 1 tablespoon reduced-sodium teriyaki sauce
- 1/2 pound ground pork
- 2 green onions, finely chopped
- 1/2 teaspoon grated fresh gingerroot
  Dash ground allspice
  Dash pepper
- 2 fresh pineapple slices (about 1/4 inch thick)
- 4 green pepper rings, thinly sliced
- 4 Hawaiian sweet rolls, split
- 2 Bibb or Boston lettuce leaves, halved

**1.** In a small bowl, mix mustard, honey and teriyaki sauce.

**2.** In a large bowl, combine the pork, green onions, ginger, allspice and pepper, mixing lightly but thoroughly. Shape into four 1/4-in.-thick patties.

**3.** Grill burgers, covered, over medium heat for 2-3 minutes on each side or until a thermometer reads 160°.

**4.** Meanwhile, brush the pineapple slices with 1 tablespoon mustard mixture. Grill 2-3 minutes on each side or until lightly browned. Grill pepper rings 1-2 minutes on each side or until crisp-tender. Cut the pineapple and pepper slices in half. Grill rolls, cut side down, for 30-60 seconds or until toasted.

**5.** Serve the burgers on rolls with lettuce, pineapple slices, pepper rings and the remaining mustard mixture.

**NUTRITION FACTS** 2 sliders equals 515 cal., 20 g fat (8 g sat. fat), 101 mg chol., 899 mg sodium, 56 g carb. (33 g sugars, 3 g fiber), 26 g pro.

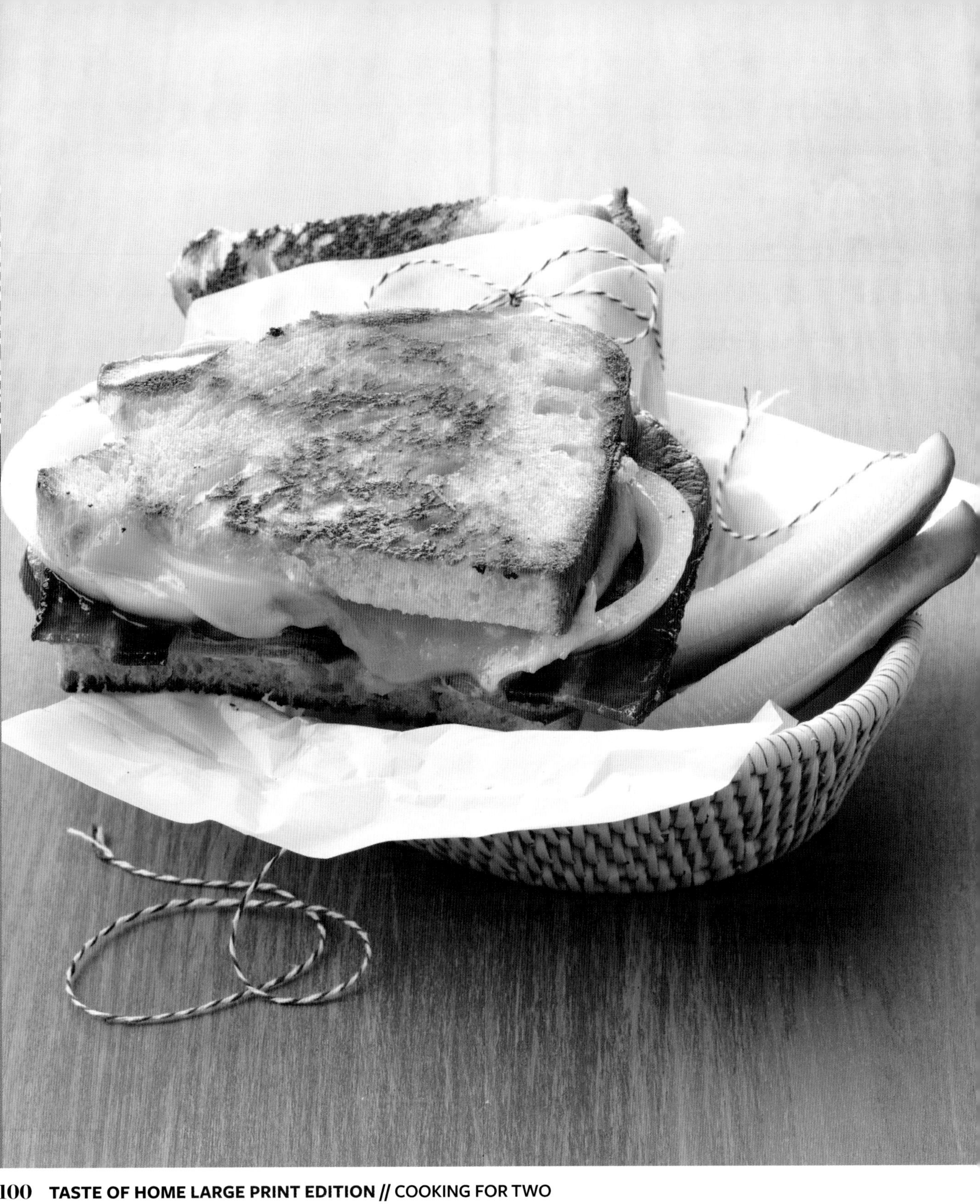

## Best-Ever Grilled Cheese Sandwiches

You can use your imagination to come up with other fillings, such as a sprinkle of Parmesan cheese, Italian seasoning or chives, or even a spoonful of salsa.

**—EDIE DESPAIN** LOGAN, UT

**START TO FINISH:** 20 MIN.
**MAKES:** 2 SERVINGS

- 2 tablespoons mayonnaise
- 1 teaspoon Dijon mustard
- 4 slices sourdough bread
- 2 slices Swiss cheese
- 2 slices cheddar cheese
- 2 slices sweet onion
- 1 medium tomato, sliced
- 6 cooked bacon strips
- 2 tablespoons butter, softened

**1.** Combine mayonnaise and mustard; spread over two bread slices. Layer with cheeses, onion, tomato and bacon; top with the remaining bread. Spread outsides of sandwiches with butter.

**2.** In a small skillet over medium heat, toast sandwiches for 2-3 minutes on each side or until the cheese is melted.

**NUTRITION FACTS** 1 serving equals 714 cal., 48 g fat (23 g sat. fat), 111 mg chol., 1291 mg sodium, 41 g carb. (4 g sugars, 3 g fiber), 29 g pro.

# Ultimate Panini

Sometimes I crave caramelized onions. I want to pair them with something special, and this sandwich is just that. It's a delicious option for lunch or dinner.

**—CHARLENE BROGAN** FALMOUTH, ME

**PREP:** 30 MIN. • **COOK:** 5 MIN./BATCH
**MAKES:** 2 SERVINGS

- 1 large onion, sliced
- 1 tablespoon canola oil
- 2 slices provolone cheese
- 1/4 pound thinly sliced deli ham
- 1 small tomato, sliced
- 4 garlic-flavored sandwich pickle slices
- 4 slices Italian bread (1/2 inch thick)
- 1 tablespoon butter, softened

**1.** In a small skillet, saute the onion in oil until softened. Reduce heat to medium-low; cook, stirring occasionally, for 30 minutes or until deep golden brown.

**2.** Layer cheese, ham, tomato, pickles and the caramelized onion on two bread slices; top with the remaining bread. Spread outsides of sandwiches with butter.

**3.** Cook on a panini maker or indoor grill for 3-4 minutes or until the bread is browned and the cheese is melted.

**NUTRITION FACTS** 1 panini equals 405 cal., 22 g fat (8 g sat. fat), 55 mg chol., 1188 mg sodium, 34 g carb. (7 g sugars, 3 g fiber), 20 g pro.

# Wonderburgers

This perfectly portioned recipe really comes in handy when I cook for just my husband and myself. The "homemade" buns make these sandwiches extra special.

**—CATHY ZADEL** HANALEI, HI

---

**START TO FINISH:** 30 MIN.
**MAKES:** 2 SERVINGS

---

### BUNS

- 1 tube (11 ounces) refrigerated breadsticks
- 1 large egg
- 1 tablespoon water
  Sesame seeds

### HAMBURGERS

- 1 large egg
- 1 to 2 tablespoons soy sauce
- ¼ cup chopped onion
- ½ to 1 teaspoon dried thyme
- ¼ teaspoon salt
- ¼ teaspoon pepper
- ⅔ pound ground beef
  Lettuce leaves

**1.** Separate breadsticks into 12 pieces. Pinch the ends of two pieces together to form a rope. Repeat to form six ropes. Shape each rope into a coil; flatten to ½-in. thickness. Stack two coils on an ungreased baking sheet. Repeat twice to make three stacks. Combine egg and water and beat to mix. Brush the egg mixture over the dough and sprinkle with sesame seeds.

**2.** Bake at 350° for 15-18 minutes or until golden brown; cool on a wire rack. Save one bun for another use.

**3.** Meanwhile, in a small bowl, combine the egg, soy sauce, onion, thyme, salt and pepper. Crumble beef over mixture and mix well; shape into two ¾-in.-thick patties. Grill, covered, over medium-high heat for 5-7 minutes on each side or until no longer pink. Split two of the buns in half; serve the burgers on the buns and top with lettuce and burgers.

**NUTRITION FACTS** 1 burger equals 641 cal., 28 g fat (11 g sat. fat), 305 mg chol., 1649 mg sodium, 53 g carb. (7 g sugars, 2 g fiber), 42 g pro.

EAT SMART

# Cilantro Bean Burgers

Seasoned with cilantro and cumin, bean patties make a tempting alternative to hamburgers. Jazz them up with a little salsa or guacamole.

**—DOROTHY ANDREWS** GRAFTON, WI

**PREP:** 15 MIN. + CHILLING • **COOK:** 10 MIN.
**MAKES:** 2 SERVINGS

½ cup canned pinto beans, rinsed and drained
½ cup canned black beans, rinsed and drained
¼ cup shredded carrots
1 tablespoon minced fresh cilantro
¾ teaspoon dried minced onion
¾ teaspoon lime juice
1 small garlic clove, minced
¼ teaspoon ground cumin
⅛ teaspoon salt
⅛ teaspoon pepper
¼ cup soft bread crumbs
2 tablespoons egg substitute
1½ teaspoons cornmeal
1½ teaspoons canola oil
Salsa, guacamole and tortilla chips, optional

**1.** In a food processor, combine the first 10 ingredients; cover and pulse until blended. Stir in bread crumbs and egg substitute; refrigerate for 30 minutes.

**2.** Shape bean mixture into two patties; sprinkle each side with cornmeal. In a large nonstick skillet, cook patties in oil for 4-5 minutes on each side or until lightly browned. If desired, serve with salsa, guacamole and tortilla chips.

**NUTRITION FACTS** 1 burger equals 177 cal., 4 g fat (0 sat. fat), 0 chol., 432 mg sodium, 26 g carb. (3 g sugars, 6 g fiber), 8 g pro. *Diabetic Exchanges:* 1½ starch, 1 lean meat, ½ fat.

**TOP TIP**

Make soft bread crumbs from fresh or slightly stale bread. Tear the bread apart with a fork, or use a blender or food processor to break it into fluffy crumbs. Pile gently into a measuring cup and do not pack.

# Chicken Gyros

These yummy Greek specialties are a cinch to prepare. Tender chicken and creamy cucumber sauce are tucked into pitas.
—*TASTE OF HOME* TEST KITCHEN

**PREP:** 20 MIN. + MARINATING
**COOK:** 10 MIN.
**MAKES:** 2 SERVINGS

- ¼ cup lemon juice
- 2 tablespoons olive oil
- ¾ teaspoon minced garlic, divided
- ½ teaspoon ground mustard
- ½ teaspoon dried oregano
- ½ pound boneless skinless chicken breasts, cut into ½-inch strips
- ½ cup chopped peeled cucumber
- ⅓ cup plain yogurt
- ¼ teaspoon dill weed
- 2 whole pita breads
- ½ small red onion, thinly sliced

**1.** In a large resealable plastic bag, combine lemon juice, oil, ½ teaspoon garlic, mustard and oregano; add chicken. Seal bag and turn to coat; refrigerate for at least 1 hour. In a small bowl, combine cucumber, yogurt, dill and the remaining garlic; cover and refrigerate until serving.

**2.** Drain the chicken and discard the marinade. In a large nonstick skillet, cook and stir the chicken for 7-8 minutes or until no longer pink. Spoon onto pita breads. Top with the yogurt mixture and sliced onion; fold in half.

**NUTRITION FACTS** 1 gyro equals 367 cal., 9 g fat (2 g sat. fat), 68 mg chol., 397 mg sodium, 39 g carb. (4 g sugars, 2 g fiber), 30 g pro. *Diabetic Exchanges:* 3 lean meat, 2½ starch, 1 fat.

**FAST FIX**

# Quick Crab Melts

Two types of cheese melted over a savory crab mixture make these open-face sandwiches amazing. I usually serve them for dinner, but you can cut them in half for a terrific appetizer.
—**DONNA BENNETT** BRAMALEA, ON

**START TO FINISH:** 15 MIN.
**MAKES:** 2 SERVINGS

- 1 can (6 ounces) crabmeat, drained, flaked and cartilage removed
- 3 tablespoons mayonnaise
- 5 teaspoons finely chopped celery
- 1 tablespoon minced green onion
- 2 English muffins, split
- 4 slices tomato
- 4 thin slices cheddar cheese
- 4 thin slices Monterey Jack cheese
  Paprika

**1.** Preheat broiler. In a small bowl, mix crab, mayonnaise, celery and green onion until blended.

**2.** Place muffin halves on an ungreased baking sheet. Broil 4-6 in. from heat until toasted. Spread each half with crab mixture. Top with tomato and cheeses; sprinkle with paprika. Broil until bubbly.

**NUTRITION FACTS** 1 serving equals 492 cal., 29 g fat (10 g sat. fat), 123 mg chol., 1055 mg sodium, 28 g carb. (3 g sugars, 3 g fiber), 29 g pro.

# Taco Salad Wraps

These fun and flavorful wraps will be a hit at lunch or dinner. You'll love the little bit of crunch from the taco chips inside.
—**MARLENE ROBERTS** MOORE, OK

**START TO FINISH:** 25 MIN.
**MAKES:** 2 SERVINGS

¼   pound lean ground beef (90% lean)
⅓   cup plus 2 tablespoons salsa, divided
¼   cup chili beans, drained
1½  teaspoons Worcestershire sauce
1   teaspoon onion powder
1   teaspoon chili powder
⅛   teaspoon garlic powder
    Pepper to taste
2   flour tortillas (8 inches), warmed
⅓   cup shredded lettuce
1   plum tomato, chopped
2   tablespoons shredded cheddar cheese
6   baked tortilla chip scoops, coarsely crushed

**1.** In a small nonstick skillet, cook beef over medium heat until no longer pink; drain. Stir in ⅓ cup salsa, chili beans, Worcestershire sauce, onion powder, chili powder, garlic powder and pepper. Bring to a boil; reduce heat and simmer, uncovered, for 5 minutes.

**2.** Spoon the meat mixture onto each tortilla. Layer with lettuce, tomato, cheese, crushed tortilla chips and the remaining salsa; roll up.

**NUTRITION FACTS** 1 wrap equals 345 cal., 10 g fat (4 g sat. fat), 35 mg chol., 764 mg sodium, 42 g carb. (3 g sugars, 5 g fiber), 20 g pro.

**TOP TIP**

Heating tortillas makes them more pliable and keeps them from tearing when rolled up. You can warm tortillas in a dry skillet on top of the stove, or wrap them in foil and put them in a 350° oven for 10-15 minutes.

**Garden Chickpea Salad,**
**p. 120**

# Sides for Two

Grains, salads, green veggies or potatoes—
these delicious side dishes are ideal choices
to set next to your favorite main course.

**Lemon-Garlic Brussels
Sprouts, p. 136**

**Summer Squash and
Tomato with Feta, p. 131**

**Potato-Stuffed
Tomatoes, p. 119**

**FAST FIX**

# Pear Harvest Salad

We created this delicious salad while using up leftover turkey after Thanksgiving. Sometimes it's enough for a whole meal.
**—NANCY PREWITT** BEAVERTON, OR

**START TO FINISH:** 25 MIN.
**MAKES:** 2 SERVINGS

- 1 package (5 ounces) spring mix salad greens
- 2 cups cubed cooked turkey breast
- 1 medium pear, sliced
- 1/2 medium ripe avocado, peeled and cubed
- 1/4 cup pomegranate seeds
- 1/4 small red onion, thinly sliced

**DRESSING**
- 3 tablespoons cider vinegar
- 2 tablespoons olive oil
- 2 tablespoons honey
- 1/2 teaspoon Dijon mustard
- 1/4 teaspoon salt
- 1/8 teaspoon pepper

**TOPPINGS**
- 1/4 cup crumbled blue cheese
- 1/4 cup honey-roasted sliced almonds

**1.** Divide spring mix between two plates. Top with turkey, pear, avocado, pomegranate seeds and onion.

**2.** Whisk the dressing ingredients; drizzle over salads. Sprinkle with cheese and almonds. Serve immediately.

**NUTRITION FACTS** 1 serving equals 673 cal., 34 g fat (7 g sat. fat), 133 mg chol., 824 mg sodium, 43 g carb. (32 g sugars, 7 g fiber), 51 g pro.

# Potato-Stuffed Tomatoes

Even veggie-fearing kids will eat these up. Be sure not to bake the tomatoes much longer than 10 minutes or they're likely to soften and fall apart.

**—TASTE OF HOME TEST KITCHEN**

---

**START TO FINISH:** 30 MIN.
**MAKES:** 2 SERVINGS

---

2 small tomatoes
1/8 teaspoon salt
1/2 cup mashed potatoes (with added milk and butter)
1 tablespoon minced fresh parsley
2 tablespoons shredded Parmesan cheese, divided
1 tablespoon chopped green onion

**1.** Cut a thin slice off the top of each tomato. Scoop out pulp, leaving a 1/4-in. shell. Sprinkle salt on the insides of the tomatoes; invert onto paper towels and let drain for 10 minutes.

**2.** In a small bowl, combine the potatoes, parsley, 1 tablespoon cheese and onion. Spoon into tomatoes. Sprinkle with remaining cheese.

**3.** Place in a small baking dish coated with cooking spray. Bake at 400° for 10 minutes or until heated through.

**NUTRITION FACTS** 1 stuffed tomato equals 98 cal., 4 g fat (2 g sat. fat), 9 mg chol., 405 mg sodium, 13 g carb. (3 g sugars, 2 g fiber), 4 g pro. *Diabetic Exchanges:* 1 vegetable, 1/2 starch, 1/2 fat.

# Garden Chickpea Salad

Looking for something different on a hot summer's day? This refreshing salad makes a terrific cold side dish or even an entree.

**—SALLY SIBTHORPE** SHELBY TOWNSHIP, MI

**START TO FINISH:** 25 MIN.
**MAKES:** 2 SERVINGS

½ teaspoon cumin seeds
¼ cup chopped tomato
¼ cup lemon juice
¼ cup olive oil
1 garlic clove, minced
¼ teaspoon salt
¼ teaspoon cayenne pepper

**SALAD**

¾ cup canned chickpeas, rinsed and drained
1 medium carrot, julienned
1 small zucchini, julienned
2 green onions, thinly sliced
½ cup coarsely chopped fresh parsley
¼ cup thinly sliced radishes
¼ cup crumbled feta cheese
3 tablespoons chopped walnuts
3 cups spring mix salad greens

**1.** For dressing, in a dry small skillet, toast cumin seeds over medium heat until aromatic, stirring frequently. Transfer to a small bowl. Stir in tomato, lemon juice, oil, garlic, salt and cayenne pepper.

**2.** In a second bowl, combine chickpeas, carrot, zucchini, green onions, parsley, radishes, cheese and walnuts. Stir in ⅓ cup dressing.

**3.** To serve, divide the salad greens between two plates or bowls; top with chickpea mixture. Drizzle with the remaining dressing.

**NUTRITION FACTS** 1 serving equals 492 cal., 38 g fat (6 g sat. fat), 8 mg chol., 619 mg sodium, 30 g carb. (7 g sugars, 9 g fiber), 12 g pro.

**DID YOU KNOW?**

Chickpeas may have been grown in Turkey as long as 7,400 years ago, and they are still one of the world's most widely consumed crops. Chickpeas grow as seeds in pods on a bushy plant—the leaves of which are used in the textile industry as a source of blue fabric dye.

# Best Spanish Rice

We love the zing from the Cajun seasoning and hot sauce. I also like to use this spicy rice to make stuffed green peppers.
—**MARY HOXWORTH** KILLBUCK, OH

---

**PREP:** 15 MIN. • **COOK:** 25 MIN.
**MAKES:** 3 SERVINGS

---

¼  pound bulk Italian sausage
3  tablespoons each chopped onion, celery and green pepper
1  small garlic clove, minced
1  cup water
⅓  cup uncooked long grain rice
⅛  teaspoon Cajun seasoning
1  to 2 drops hot pepper sauce
   Dash each salt, paprika and pepper
¾  cup canned diced tomatoes

**1.** In a small saucepan, cook the sausage, onion, celery and green pepper over medium heat until meat is no longer pink and the vegetables are tender. Add garlic; cook 1 minute longer. Drain.

**2.** Add the water, rice, Cajun seasoning, pepper sauce, salt, paprika and pepper; bring to a boil. Reduce heat; cover and simmer for 20 minutes or until rice is tender, stirring once. Stir in tomatoes; heat through.

**NUTRITION FACTS** ⅔ cup equals 158 cal., 5 g fat (2 g sat. fat), 15 mg chol., 342 mg sodium, 22 g carb. (3 g sugars, 2 g fiber), 6 g pro. *Diabetic Exchanges:* 1 starch, 1 vegetable, 1 fat.

# Zucchini Fries

I often make these fries for my husband and myself, especially when our garden is full of zucchini. The cornmeal coating gives them a nice crunch.

—**SARAH GOTTSCHALK** RICHMOND, IN

**START TO FINISH:** 30 MIN.
**MAKES:** 2 SERVINGS

- 2 small zucchini
- 1 large egg white
- ¼ cup all-purpose flour
- 3 tablespoons cornmeal
- ½ teaspoon each salt, garlic powder, chili powder, paprika and pepper
  Cooking spray
  Marinara or spaghetti sauce, warmed

**1.** Cut zucchini into 3x½x½-in. pieces. In a shallow bowl, whisk egg white. In another shallow bowl, combine the flour, cornmeal and seasonings. Dip zucchini in egg white, then roll in flour mixture.

**2.** Place zucchini on a baking sheet coated with cooking spray; spray with additional cooking spray. Bake at 425° for 18-22 minutes or until golden brown, turning once. Serve with marinara sauce.

**NUTRITION FACTS** 1 serving equals 98 cal., 1 g fat (0 sat. fat), 0 chol., 414 mg sodium, 19 g carb. (3 g sugars, 3 g fiber), 5 g pro. *Diabetic Exchanges:* 1 starch, 1 vegetable.

**(5) INGREDIENTS** **FAST FIX**

## Chipotle Smashed Sweet Potatoes

This smoky, buttery sweet potato mash is simply divine. The chipotle pairs nicely with the spuds, and the creamy texture is delightful.

**—DANIELLE WILLIAMS** WESTVILLE, OK

---

**START TO FINISH:** 30 MIN.
**MAKES:** 2 SERVINGS

---

- 1   large sweet potato, peeled and quartered
- 1   tablespoon 2% milk
- 2   teaspoons butter
- 1   teaspoon minced chipotle pepper in adobo sauce
- 1/8 teaspoon salt
      Dash pepper

**1.** Place sweet potato in a small saucepan and cover with water. Bring to a boil. Reduce heat; cover and simmer for 15-20 minutes or until tender.

**2.** Drain potato and return to the pan. Add milk, butter, chipotle pepper, salt and pepper; coarsely mash.

**NUTRITION FACTS** 2/3 cup equals 136 cal., 4 g fat (3 g sat. fat), 11 mg chol., 219 mg sodium, 23 g carb. (10 g sugars, 3 g fiber), 2 g pro.

EAT SMART **FAST FIX**

## Sweet Peas Parma

This is a simple side with delicious Italian flavors. Peas get dressed up for dinner with just a few easy additions. Don't skip this one!

**—JILL ANDERSON** SLEEPY EYE, MN

**START TO FINISH:** 20 MIN.
**MAKES:** 2 SERVINGS

- 1¾ cups frozen peas
- 2 thin slices prosciutto or deli ham, coarsely chopped
- ½ teaspoon minced garlic
- 1½ teaspoons olive oil
- 1½ teaspoons butter
- 1 small tomatoes, seeded and chopped
- ⅛ teaspoon salt
  Dash pepper

**1.** Place peas in a steamer basket; place in a large saucepan over 1 in. of water. Bring to a boil; cover and steam for 4 minutes.

**2.** Meanwhile, in a large skillet, cook prosciutto and garlic in oil and butter over medium heat until prosciutto is crisp. Add the tomato, salt and pepper; heat through. Stir in peas.

**NUTRITION FACTS** ¾ cup equals 192 cal., 9 g fat (3 g sat. fat), 20 mg chol., 584 mg sodium, 19 g carb. (8 g sugars, 7 g fiber), 11 g pro. *Diabetic Exchanges:* 1 starch, 1 lean meat, 1 fat.

## Summer Squash and Tomato with Feta

You can enjoy this dish while the squash is still warm, but it also tastes great cold. You'll love how it captures the fresh flavors and bright colors of summer.

**—RANI LONG** COLD SPRING, NY

---

**START TO FINISH:** 20 MIN.
**MAKES:** 2 SERVINGS

---

1  medium yellow summer squash, thinly sliced
1  tablespoon lemon juice
1  tablespoon olive oil
2  teaspoons snipped fresh dill or ½ teaspoon dill weed
1  small garlic clove, minced
½  teaspoon Dijon mustard
¼  teaspoon sugar
¼  teaspoon salt
⅛  teaspoon pepper
¼  cup crumbled feta cheese
1  medium tomato, diced
¼  cup finely chopped sweet onion

**1.** In a small saucepan, bring ½ in. of water to a boil. Add squash; cover and boil for 3-4 minutes or until tender. Drain.

**2.** In a large bowl, combine lemon juice, oil, dill, garlic, mustard, sugar, salt and pepper. Gently stir in the squash and cheese. Transfer to a serving platter. Combine tomato and onion; spoon over the squash mixture. Serve immediately.

**NUTRITION FACTS** 1 cup equals 140 cal., 9 g fat (3 g sat. fat), 8 mg chol., 467 mg sodium, 11 g carb. (6 g sugars, 3 g fiber), 5 g pro.

**EAT SMART** **⑤ INGREDIENTS** **FAST FIX** ▶

## Super Spinach Salad

Thanks to this recipe, an elegant salad is a cinch to make. Good-for-you spinach is the perfect backdrop for salty bacon bits and tangy balsamic vinaigrette.

**—MARY "PEGGY" HARRIS** SHIVELY, KY

**START TO FINISH:** 10 MIN.
**MAKES:** 2 SERVINGS

1½ cups fresh baby spinach
¾ cup sliced fresh mushrooms
½ hard-cooked large egg, chopped
4½ teaspoons real bacon bits
2 tablespoons balsamic vinaigrette

In a small salad bowl, combine the spinach, mushrooms, egg and bacon. Drizzle with vinaigrette; toss to coat.

**NUTRITION FACTS** 1 cup equals 79 cal., 5 g fat (1 g sat. fat), 57 mg chol., 327 mg sodium, 4 g carb. (2 g sugars, 1 g fiber), 5 g pro. *Diabetic Exchanges:* 1 vegetable, 1 fat.

## Tangy Baked Beans

Different, delicious and sized exactly right for two people, this easy home-style side dish is sure to please.

**—DEAN COPELAND** OCHLOCKNEE, GA

---

**PREP:** 10 MIN. • **BAKE:** 25 MIN.
**MAKES:** 2 SERVINGS

---

- 2 bacon strips, cut into 1-inch pieces
- 2 tablespoons strong brewed coffee
- 4 teaspoons brown sugar
- 1 teaspoon cider vinegar
- 1/4 teaspoon ground mustard
- 1/8 teaspoon salt
- 1 can (8.3 ounces) baked beans, undrained
- 1/2 cup chopped onion

**1.** In a small skillet, cook bacon over medium heat until partially cooked but not crisp. Drain on paper towels. Meanwhile, in a small saucepan, combine the coffee, brown sugar, vinegar, mustard and salt. Bring to a boil; cook and stir for 2-3 minutes or until sugar is dissolved. Stir in beans and onion.

**2.** Divide the bean mixture between two 6-oz. ramekins or custard cups coated with cooking spray. Top with bacon. Bake at 350° for 25-30 minutes or until bubbly.

**NUTRITION FACTS** 1/2 cup equals 213 cal., 5 g fat (2 g sat. fat), 14 mg chol., 741 mg sodium, 36 g carb. (19 g sugars, 7 g fiber), 9 g pro. *Diabetic Exchanges:* 2 starch, 1 vegetable, 1/2 lean meat.

**EAT SMART** (5) **INGREDIENTS** **FAST FIX**

## Lemon-Garlic Brussels Sprouts

Even lifelong Brussels sprouts haters love these. For a heartier dish, I sometimes add crumbled bacon.
—**JAN ROBERTS** SAN PEDRO, CA

**START TO FINISH:** 30 MIN.
**MAKES:** 2 SERVINGS

- ½ pound fresh Brussels sprouts
- 1½ teaspoons olive oil
- 1½ teaspoons lemon juice
- ¼ teaspoon salt
- ¼ teaspoon garlic powder
  Dash pepper
- 1 tablespoon shredded Parmesan cheese

**1.** Cut an "X" in the base of each Brussels sprout. Place Brussels sprouts in a shallow baking pan coated with cooking spray. Drizzle with oil and lemon juice; sprinkle with salt, garlic powder and pepper.

**2.** Bake, uncovered, at 400° for 20-25 minutes or until tender, stirring once. Sprinkle with cheese.

**NUTRITION FACTS** ¾ cup equals 91 cal., 4 g fat (1 g sat. fat), 2 mg chol., 366 mg sodium, 11 g carb. (3 g sugars, 4 g fiber), 5 g protein. *Diabetic Exchanges:* 2 vegetable, 1 fat.

# Hoppin' John

A New Year's tradition, this mildly flavored rice dish is a great accompaniment to almost any entree.

**—BETH WALL** INMAN, SC

**START TO FINISH:** 15 MIN.
**MAKES:** 2 SERVINGS

¼ cup chopped sweet red pepper
¼ cup chopped green pepper
2 tablespoons chopped onion
¼ teaspoon garlic powder
⅛ teaspoon salt
1 tablespoon butter
⅔ cup canned black-eyed peas, rinsed and drained
⅔ cup cooked rice

In a small skillet, saute the peppers, onion, garlic powder and salt in butter for 4-5 minutes or until vegetables are tender. Stir in the peas and rice; heat through, stirring occasionally.

**NUTRITION FACTS** ¾ cup equals 194 cal., 6 g fat (4 g sat. fat), 15 mg chol., 374 mg sodium, 29 g carb. (2 g sugars, 3 g fiber), 6 g pro. *Diabetic Exchanges:* 1½ starch, 1 vegetable, 1 fat.

FAST FIX ▶
# Thai-Style Green Beans

Two for Thai, anyone? Peanut butter, soy and hoisin sauce flavor this quick and fabulous bean dish.
**—CANDACE MCMENAMIN** LEXINGTON, SC

**START TO FINISH:** 20 MIN.
**MAKES:** 2 SERVINGS

- 1 tablespoon reduced-sodium soy sauce
- 1 tablespoon hoisin sauce
- 1 tablespoon creamy peanut butter
- 1/8 teaspoon crushed red pepper flakes
- 1 tablespoon chopped shallot
- 1 teaspoon minced fresh gingerroot
- 1 tablespoon canola oil
- 1/2 pound fresh green beans, trimmed
  Minced fresh cilantro and chopped dry roasted peanuts, optional

**1.** In a small bowl, combine soy sauce, hoisin sauce, peanut butter and red pepper flakes; set aside.

**2.** In a small skillet, saute shallot and ginger in oil over medium heat for 2 minutes or until crisp-tender. Add green beans; cook and stir for 3 minutes or until crisp-tender. Add the sauce; toss to coat. Sprinkle with cilantro and peanuts if desired.

**NUTRITION FACTS** 1 cup equals 168 cal., 12 g fat (1 g sat. fat), 0 chol., 476 mg sodium, 14 g carb. (3 g sugars, 4 g fiber), 5 g pro.

**Saucy Beef with Broccoli, p. 159**

# Beef for Two

Steak or stir-fry, pies or pasta, meat loaf
or savory stew—make hearty beef
the center of your homemade meal!

**Feta Stuffed
Peppers, p. 167**

**Tender Beef over
Noodles, p. 152**

**Cranberry Short
Ribs, p. 144**

# Cranberry Short Ribs

This recipe originally came from my mother-in-law. Living in the bush in the Yukon, I sometimes substitute moose for the beef, and I pick wild cranberries in the fall. I prepare this comfort food often during the long winter months here, and we never tire of it.

**—CATHY WYLIE** DAWSON CITY, YT

**PREP:** 20 MIN. • **BAKE:** 1½ HOURS
**MAKES:** 2 SERVINGS

| | |
|---|---|
| 1½ | pounds bone-in beef short ribs |
| ½ | teaspoon salt, divided |
| ¼ | teaspoon pepper |
| 1 | tablespoon all-purpose flour |
| 1 | tablespoon brown sugar |
| ⅛ | teaspoon ground mustard |
| | Dash ground cloves |
| ¾ | cup water |
| 2 | teaspoons cider vinegar |
| ½ | cup fresh or frozen cranberries |
| 1½ | to 2 teaspoons grated lemon peel |
| ½ | teaspoon browning sauce, optional |

**1.** Preheat oven to 350°. Place ribs in a greased 8-in. square baking dish; sprinkle with ¼ teaspoon salt and pepper. Bake, covered, until tender, 1¼-1½ hours.

**2.** In a small saucepan, combine flour, brown sugar, mustard, cloves and the remaining salt; gradually whisk in water and vinegar until smooth. Stir in cranberries, lemon peel and, if desired, browning sauce; bring to a boil. Cook and stir until thickened, about 2 minutes.

**3.** Drain ribs. Pour cranberry mixture over the ribs. Bake, uncovered, for 15 minutes longer.

**NOTE** This recipe can be easily doubled to serve 4; bake in a greased 11x7-in. baking dish and increase covered baking time to 1½-1¾ hours or until tender.

**NUTRITION FACTS** 1 serving equals 314 cal., 16 g fat (7 g sat. fat), 82 mg chol., 645 mg sodium, 13 g carb. (8 g sugars, 1 g fiber), 28 g pro.

# Steaks with Poblano Relish

Spice up mealtime with these juicy tenderloin steaks topped with a zippy Southwest-style poblano pepper and garlic relish.

**—BILLIE MOSS** WALNUT CREEK, CA

**PREP:** 10 MIN. + STANDING • **COOK:** 10 MIN.
**MAKES:** 2 SERVINGS

- ½ poblano or Anaheim pepper, stem and seeds removed
- 1 unpeeled garlic clove
- 1 teaspoon minced fresh cilantro
- ½ teaspoon ground cumin, divided
- ⅛ teaspoon plus ¼ teaspoon chili powder, divided
- 2 beef tenderloin steaks (4 ounces each)
- 1 teaspoon olive oil
  Dash salt and pepper

**1.** Broil pepper half and garlic clove 4 in. from heat until the skin on the pepper blisters, about 10-12 minutes. Immediately place pepper and garlic in a bowl; cover and let stand 15-20 minutes.

**2.** Peel the pepper and garlic; finely chop and place in a small bowl. Stir in cilantro, ¼ teaspoon cumin and ⅛ teaspoon chili powder; set aside.

**3.** Rub steaks with oil. Combine salt, pepper and remaining cumin and chili powder; rub over steaks. In a nonstick skillet, cook the steaks over medium-high heat 5-7 minutes on each side or until the meat reaches desired doneness (for medium-rare, a meat thermometer should read 145°; medium, 160°; well-done, 170°). Let stand 5 minutes. Serve with the poblano relish.

**NOTE** Wear disposable gloves when cutting hot peppers; the oils can burn skin. Avoid touching your face.

**NUTRITION FACTS** 1 steak with 2 tablespoons relish equals 208 cal., 11 g fat (3 g sat. fat), 71 mg chol., 133 mg sodium, 3 g carb. (1 g sugars, 1 g fiber), 24 g pro. *Diabetic Exchanges:* 3 lean meat, ½ fat.

# Greek-Style Ravioli

Here's a flavorful Greek twist on an Italian classic. It's an easy weekday meal that's become one of our favorites. My husband and I enjoy it with garlic cheese toast.

**—HETTI WILLIAMS** RAPID CITY, SD

**START TO FINISH:** 25 MIN.
**MAKES:** 2 SERVINGS

12  frozen cheese ravioli
1/3  pound lean ground beef (90% lean)
 1  cup canned diced tomatoes with basil, oregano and garlic
 1  cup fresh baby spinach
1/4  cup sliced ripe olives
1/4  cup crumbled feta cheese

**1.** Cook ravioli according to package directions; drain. Meanwhile, in a skillet, cook beef over medium heat 4-6 minutes or until no longer pink; drain. Stir in tomatoes; bring to a boil. Reduce heat; simmer, uncovered, 10 minutes, stirring occasionally.

**2.** Add the ravioli, spinach and olives; heat through, stirring gently to combine. Sprinkle with cheese.

**NUTRITION FACTS** 1¼ cups equals 333 cal., 12 g fat (5 g sat. fat), 61 mg chol., 851 mg sodium, 28 g carb. (5 g sugars, 4 g fiber), 23 g pro. *Diabetic Exchanges:* 3 lean meat, 2 starch, ½ fat.

# Home-Style Hearty Meat Pie

This savory meat pie is a sure way to warm up any cold winter night. Chuck steak, vegetables and seasonings do the trick.
—*TASTE OF HOME* TEST KITCHEN

**PREP:** 25 MIN. • **BAKE:** 40 MIN.
**MAKES:** 2 SERVINGS

- 1   boneless beef chuck steak ($\frac{1}{2}$ pound), cut into $\frac{1}{4}$-inch cubes
- 1   teaspoon canola oil
- 2   tablespoons brown gravy mix
- $\frac{1}{2}$   cup plus 1 teaspoon water, divided
- 1   medium potato, peeled and diced
- 1   medium carrot, peeled and diced
- $\frac{1}{4}$   cup chopped onion
- 1   tablespoon minced fresh parsley
- 1   garlic clove, minced
- $\frac{1}{4}$   teaspoon salt
- $\frac{1}{4}$   teaspoon dried thyme
- $\frac{1}{4}$   teaspoon pepper
- $\frac{1}{8}$   teaspoon rubbed sage
- 1   sheet refrigerated pie pastry
- 1   tablespoon beaten egg

**1.** In a small skillet, brown beef in oil; set aside. In a small microwave-safe bowl, combine gravy mix and $\frac{1}{2}$ cup water. Microwave on high for 1-2 minutes or until thickened, stirring frequently. In a large bowl, combine the beef, potato, carrot, onion, parsley, garlic and seasonings; stir in 1 tablespoon gravy. Set aside the remaining gravy.

**2.** Place pastry on a baking sheet coated with cooking spray. Spoon the meat mixture over half of the pastry. Fold the pastry over filling and seal the edges tightly with a fork; cut slits in the top. Combine egg and remaining water; brush over top.

**3.** Bake at 375° for 40-45 minutes or until golden brown. Warm the reserved gravy; serve with the meat pie.

**NUTRITION FACTS** 1 serving equals 813 cal., 42 g fat (16 g sat. fat), 106 mg chol., 1341 mg sodium, 77 g carb. (9 g sugars, 2 g fiber), 30 g pro.

# Tender Beef over Noodles

I dress up thrifty stew meat with noodles and sweet red sauce for this satisfying main dish. It goes beautifully with salad and garlic bread.
—**OLIVIA GUST** SALEM, OR

**PREP:** 15 MIN. • **COOK:** 5½ HOURS
**MAKES:** 2 SERVINGS

½ to ¾ pound beef stew meat
⅓ cup chopped onion
1 teaspoon canola oil
1 cup water, divided
⅓ cup ketchup
1 tablespoon brown sugar
1 tablespoon Worcestershire sauce
½ teaspoon paprika
¼ teaspoon ground mustard
3 tablespoons all-purpose flour
1 cup uncooked egg noodles
  Minced fresh parsley, optional

**1.** In a small skillet, brown beef and onion in oil; drain. Transfer to a 1½-qt. slow cooker.

**2.** In a small bowl, combine ½ cup water, ketchup, brown sugar, Worcestershire sauce, paprika and mustard; pour over meat. Cover and cook on low for 5 hours or until the meat is tender.

**3.** Combine flour and the remaining water until smooth; stir into the meat mixture. Cover and cook 30 minutes longer or until thickened.

**4.** Meanwhile, cook noodles according to package directions; drain. Stir in parsley if desired. Serve with the beef.

**NUTRITION FACTS** 1½ cups equals 385 cal., 11 g fat (3 g sat. fat), 89 mg chol., 611 mg sodium, 44 g carb. (13 g sugars, 2 g fiber), 27 g pro.

**TOP TIP**

You can substitute a different supporting ingredient in this dish, if you prefer. Instead of egg noodles, try serving the beef over rice or ladling it over mashed potatoes.

**BEEF FOR TWO**

# Maple & Blue Cheese Steak

This is a wonderful, cheesy recipe that melts in your mouth. I love this traditional Canadian meal!

**—SUSAN JERROTT** BEDFORD, NS

**PREP:** 20 MIN. + MARINATING
**GRILL:** 10 MIN.
**MAKES:** 2 SERVINGS

- 6 tablespoons balsamic vinegar
- 6 tablespoons maple syrup, divided
- 2 tablespoons plus 1½ teaspoons Dijon mustard
- 1 tablespoon minced fresh thyme or ¼ teaspoon dried thyme
- ½ pound beef top sirloin steak
- 2 tablespoons chopped pecans
- 1½ teaspoons olive oil
- ⅛ teaspoon salt
- ⅛ teaspoon pepper
- ¼ cup crumbled blue cheese

**1.** In a small bowl, combine vinegar, 5 tablespoons of the maple syrup, the mustard and thyme. Pour ⅔ cup of the marinade into a large resealable plastic bag; add steak. Seal bag and turn to coat; refrigerate for up to 3 hours. Cover and refrigerate the remaining marinade.

**2.** Meanwhile, in a small skillet, saute pecans in oil until toasted. Stir in the remaining maple syrup. Bring to a boil; cook for 1 minute, stirring constantly. Remove from skillet and spread onto waxed paper to cool completely.

**3.** Drain and discard the marinade. Sprinkle the steak with salt and pepper. Grill, over medium heat, for 4-6 minutes on each side or until the meat reaches desired doneness (for medium-rare, a thermometer should read 145°; medium, 160°; well-done, 170°). Let stand for 5 minutes before slicing.

**4.** Place the reserved marinade in a small saucepan. Bring to a boil; cook until the liquid is reduced to ¼ cup, about 2 minutes. Divide the steak slices between two plates. Drizzle with sauce; sprinkle with blue cheese and pecans.

**NUTRITION FACTS** 1 serving equals 475 cal., 23 g fat (8 g sat. fat), 86 mg chol., 689 mg sodium, 38 g carb. (31 g sugars, 1 g fiber), 29 g pro.

# Beef Macaroni Skillet

This stovetop favorite is tasty and stick-to-your-ribs.
It's easy to prepare—perfect for after a long day at work.
—**CARMEN EDWARDS** MIDLAND, TX

---

**PREP:** 15 MIN. • **COOK:** 30 MIN.
**MAKES:** 2 SERVINGS

---

½    pound lean ground beef (90% lean)
⅓    cup chopped onion
¼    cup chopped green pepper
1½  cups Spicy Hot V8 juice
½    cup uncooked elbow macaroni
1    teaspoon Worcestershire sauce
¼    teaspoon pepper

In a large skillet, cook beef, onion and green pepper over medium heat until the meat is no longer pink; drain. Stir in the remaining ingredients. Bring to a boil. Reduce heat; cover and simmer for 18-20 minutes or until the macaroni is tender.

**NUTRITION FACTS** 1¼ cups equals 291 cal., 9 g fat (4 g sat. fat), 56 mg chol., 689 mg sodium, 25 g carb. (8 g sugars, 2 g fiber), 26 g pro. *Diabetic Exchanges:* 3 lean meat, 2 vegetable, 1 starch.

# Saucy Beef with Broccoli

When I'm looking for a fast entree, I turn to this beef and broccoli stir-fry. It features a tantalizing sauce made with garlic and ginger.

**—ROSA EVANS** ODESSA, MO

**START TO FINISH:** 30 MIN.
**MAKES:** 2 SERVINGS

- 1 tablespoon cornstarch
- ½ cup reduced-sodium beef broth
- ¼ cup sherry or additional beef broth
- 2 tablespoons reduced-sodium soy sauce
- 1 tablespoon brown sugar
- 1 garlic clove, minced
- 1 teaspoon minced fresh gingerroot
- 2 teaspoons canola oil, divided
- ½ pound beef top sirloin steak, cut into ¼-inch strips
- 2 cups fresh broccoli florets
- 8 green onions, cut into 1-inch pieces

**1.** In a small bowl, mix the first seven ingredients. In a large nonstick skillet, heat 1 teaspoon oil over medium-high heat. Add beef; stir-fry 1-2 minutes or until no longer pink. Remove from pan.

**2.** Stir-fry broccoli in remaining oil 4-5 minutes or until crisp-tender. Add green onions; cook 1-2 minutes longer or just until tender.

**3.** Stir cornstarch mixture and add to pan. Bring to a boil; cook and stir for 2-3 minutes or until thickened. Return beef to pan; heat through.

**NUTRITION FACTS** 1¼ cups equals 313 cal., 11 g fat (3 g sat. fat), 68 mg chol., 816 mg sodium, 20 g carb. (11 g sugars, 4 g fiber), 29 g pro. *Diabetic Exchanges:* 3 lean meat, 1 starch, 1 vegetable, 1 fat.

## Marinated Sirloin Steaks

Asian and Mediterranean influences meet in this sweet-spicy marinade. The blend of honey and soy sauce really works well with olive oil and balsamic vinegar. The marinade is also great for grilling New York strip steaks.

**—SARAH VASQUES** MILFORD, NH

**PREP:** 10 MIN. + MARINATING
**GRILL:** 10 MIN.
**MAKES:** 2 SERVINGS

- ¼ cup honey
- 3 tablespoons reduced-sodium soy sauce
- 2 tablespoons olive oil
- 1 tablespoon balsamic vinegar
- 2 garlic cloves, peeled
- ¼ teaspoon coarsely ground pepper
- 2 beef top sirloin steaks (4 ounces each)
- 3 green onions, sliced

**1.** In a blender, combine honey, soy sauce, oil, vinegar, garlic and pepper; cover and process until blended. Pour ⅓ cup of marinade into a large resealable plastic bag; add steaks and onions. Seal bag and turn to coat; refrigerate for at least 1-2 hours. Cover and refrigerate remaining marinade for basting.

**2.** Drain the steaks and discard their marinade. On a greased grill rack, grill the steaks, covered, over medium-hot heat, or broil 4 in. from the heat for 4-5 minutes on each side or until the meat reaches desired doneness (for medium-rare, a meat thermometer should read 145°; medium, 160°; well-done, 170°), basting occasionally with reserved marinade.

**NUTRITION FACTS** ¼ pound equals 287 cal., 12 g fat (3 g sat. fat), 63 mg chol., 506 mg sodium, 21 g carb. (18 g sugars, 1 g fiber), 23 g pro. *Diabetic Exchanges:* 3 lean meat, 1½ fruit, 1 fat.

# Sweet Potato Shepherd's Pie

When I was a child, shepherd's pie was one of my favorite meals. I made our family recipe healthier with sweet potato instead of white, then changed the veggies and spices to complement the sweet potato topping.
—**TANYA MARCKETTI** GOLDEN, CO

**PREP:** 25 MIN. • **BAKE:** 25 MIN.
**MAKES:** 2 SERVINGS

- 1 large sweet potato
- ½ pound lean ground beef (90% lean)
- ¼ cup chopped onion
- 1 can (8¾ ounces) whole kernel corn, drained
- ½ cup tomato sauce
  Dash each ground cinnamon, allspice and nutmeg
- 1 tablespoon butter
- 1 tablespoon 2% milk
- ⅛ teaspoon salt
- ⅛ teaspoon pepper

**1.** Scrub and pierce sweet potato; place on a microwave-safe plate. Microwave, uncovered, on high for 10-12 minutes or until tender, turning once.

**2.** Meanwhile, in a large skillet, cook beef and onion until the meat is no longer pink; drain. Add corn, tomato sauce and spices. Place in a 1-qt. baking dish coated with cooking spray; set aside.

**3.** When the potato is cool enough to handle, cut it in half; scoop out the pulp and place in a small bowl. Mash with butter, milk, salt and pepper. Spread evenly over the meat mixture.

**4.** Bake, uncovered, at 350° for 25-30 minutes or until heated through.

**NOTE** This recipe was tested in a 1,100-watt microwave.

**NUTRITION FACTS** 1¾ cups equals 404 cal., 12 g fat (5 g sat. fat), 64 mg chol., 900 mg sodium, 42 g carb. (16 g sugars, 6 g fiber), 27 g pro.

EAT SMART

# Skillet Pasta

This is always a good recipe to prepare when time is short. Herbs delectably lace the simple one-pot spaghetti.

**—MARV SALTER** WEST HILLS, CA

**PREP:** 15 MIN. • **COOK:** 20 MIN.
**MAKES:** 2 SERVINGS

½ pound lean ground beef (90% lean)
1 cup sliced fresh mushrooms
⅓ cup chopped onion
1 garlic clove, minced
1 cup reduced-sodium beef broth
⅔ cup water
⅓ cup tomato paste
½ teaspoon dried basil
½ teaspoon dried oregano
⅛ teaspoon pepper
3 ounces uncooked spaghetti, broken in half
2 teaspoons grated Parmesan cheese

**1.** In a large skillet, cook beef, mushrooms, onion and garlic over medium heat until the meat is no longer pink and the vegetables are tender; drain.

**2.** Stir in broth, water, tomato paste, seasonings and spaghetti. Bring to a boil. Reduce heat; cover and simmer for 15-20 minutes or until the spaghetti is tender. Sprinkle with cheese.

**NUTRITION FACTS** 1½ cups equals 414 cal., 11 g fat (4 g sat. fat), 75 mg chol., 337 mg sodium, 45 g carb. (7 g sugars, 4 g fiber), 33 g pro. *Diabetic Exchanges:* 3 lean meat, 2 starch, 2 vegetable.

# Feta Stuffed Peppers

One of my favorite meals when I was younger was my mother's chili rice casserole. I've put a Greek spin on it and stuffed it in a pepper. It works great alongside a garden salad and fresh bread.

**—SACHA MORGAN** WOODSTOCK, GA

---

**PREP:** 35 MIN. • **BAKE:** 30 MIN.
**MAKES:** 3 SERVINGS

---

3 large green peppers
1/2 pound lean ground beef (90% lean)
1 small onion, chopped
1 can (14 1/2 ounces) diced tomatoes, undrained
2 cups chopped fresh spinach
3/4 cup uncooked whole wheat orzo pasta
2 tablespoons minced fresh oregano or 2 teaspoons dried oregano
1/4 teaspoon salt
1/4 teaspoon pepper
6 tablespoons crumbled feta cheese

**1.** Cut peppers in half lengthwise and remove seeds. In a Dutch oven, cook the peppers in boiling water for 3-5 minutes. Drain and rinse in cold water; invert onto paper towels.

**2.** In a large skillet, cook beef and onion over medium heat until the meat is no longer pink. Stir in tomatoes, spinach, orzo, oregano, salt and pepper. Bring to a boil. Reduce heat; cover and simmer for 5-7 minutes or until the orzo is tender.

**3.** Spoon beef mixture into the peppers. Place filled peppers in an 11x7-in. baking dish coated with cooking spray. Cover and bake at 350° for 30-35 minutes or until the peppers are tender.

**4.** Sprinkle with cheese; bake 5 minutes longer or until the cheese is softened.

**NUTRITION FACTS** 2 stuffed pepper halves equals 369 cal., 10 g fat (4 g sat. fat), 55 mg chol., 567 mg sodium, 46 g carb. (9 g sugars, 13 g fiber), 26 g pro. *Diabetic Exchanges:* 3 starch, 2 lean meat, 1/2 fat.

EAT SMART

# Mom's Meat Loaf

I whip up this delicious loaf when I'm looking for a downsized main course. We love the pleasant sage flavor and scrumptious sauce. Plus, it's easy to double the recipe to make sandwiches the next day.

—**MICHELLE BERAN** CLAFLIN, KS

**PREP:** 15 MIN. • **BAKE:** 40 MIN.
**MAKES:** 2 MINI MEAT LOAVES

- 1 large egg
- ¼ cup 2% milk
- ⅓ cup crushed saltines
- 3 tablespoons chopped onion
- ¼ teaspoon salt
- ⅛ teaspoon rubbed sage
  Dash pepper
- ½ pound lean ground beef (90% lean)
- ¼ cup ketchup
- 2 tablespoons brown sugar
- ¼ teaspoon Worcestershire sauce

**1.** In a large bowl, beat egg. Add milk, cracker crumbs, onion, salt, sage and pepper. Crumble beef over the egg mixture and mix well. Shape into two loaves; place in a shallow baking dish coated with cooking spray.

**2.** Combine ketchup, brown sugar and Worcestershire sauce; spoon over the meat loaves. Bake at 350° for 40-45 minutes or until the meat is no longer pink and a thermometer reads 160°.

**NUTRITION FACTS** 1 loaf equals 337 cal., 12 g fat (4 g sat. fat), 162 mg chol., 898 mg sodium, 31 g carb. (18 g sugars, 1 g fiber), 27 g pro. *Diabetic Exchanges:* 3 lean meat, 2 starch.

**TOP TIP**

Although it's just the two of us, I buy family packs of ground beef to save money. I divide each pack into ¼- or ½-pound portions to freeze for use in casseroles, hamburgers and meatballs.

—**KRISTIN MCPHERSON** MOULTRIE, GA

**Chicken Reuben Roll-Ups, p. 195**

# Poultry for Two

Among the most versatile main ingredients, chicken and turkey can go from weeknight dinner to weekend date night with ease.

**Grilled Turkey Herbed Tenderloins, p. 179**

**Santa Fe Chicken Pita Pizzas, p. 191**

**Chicken Mexican Manicotti, p. 196**

**FAST FIX** ▶

# Thai Chicken Pasta

I try to buy fresh chicken when it's on sale. I cook a big batch in the slow cooker, then cut it up and package it in small amounts suitable for recipes like this. When I want it, I just need to be pull it out of the freezer and let it thaw.

**—JENI PITTARD** STATHAM, GA

---

**START TO FINISH:** 25 MIN.
**MAKES:** 2 SERVINGS

---

| | |
|---|---|
| 3 | ounces uncooked whole wheat linguine |
| ½ | cup salsa |
| 2 | tablespoons reduced-fat creamy peanut butter |
| 1 | tablespoon orange juice |
| 1½ | teaspoons honey |
| 1 | teaspoon reduced-sodium soy sauce |
| 1 | cup cubed cooked chicken breast |
| 1 | tablespoon chopped unsalted peanuts |
| 1 | tablespoon minced fresh cilantro |

**1.** Cook linguine according to package directions.

**2.** Meanwhile, in a microwave-safe dish, combine salsa, peanut butter, orange juice, honey and soy sauce. Cover and microwave on high for 1 minute; stir. Add chicken; heat through.

**3.** Drain the linguine. Serve with the chicken mixture. Garnish with peanuts and cilantro.

**NOTE** This recipe was tested in a 1,100-watt microwave.

**NUTRITION FACTS** 1 serving equals 409 cal., 10 g fat (2 g sat. fat), 54 mg chol., 474 mg sodium, 46 g carb. (10 g sugars, 6 g fiber), 33 g pro.

# Cashew Chicken

Crunchy cashews, tender chicken, celery and mushrooms make this a filling and easy-to-prepare stir-fry. The dish is a big hit with my wife and me.

**—RICHARD BORCHERS** WAUWATOSA, WI

**PREP:** 25 MIN. • **COOK:** 15 MIN.
**MAKES:** 2 SERVINGS

- 2   tablespoons reduced-sodium soy sauce
- 1   tablespoon cornstarch
- 1/4 teaspoon sugar
- 1/4 teaspoon salt
- 1/4 teaspoon ground ginger
- 2   celery ribs, sliced
- 1   medium onion, halved and sliced
- 5   teaspoons canola oil, divided
- 2   boneless skinless chicken breast halves (4 ounces each)
- 1/2 cup frozen peas
- 1/2 cup chicken broth
- 1   can (4 ounces) mushroom stems and pieces, drained
- 1/3 cup lightly salted cashews, toasted
- 1   cup hot cooked rice

**1.** In a small bowl, combine the first five ingredients until smooth; set aside.

**2.** In a large skillet, saute celery and onion in 2 teaspoons oil until tender. Remove and keep warm.

**3.** In the same skillet over medium heat, cook chicken in the remaining oil for 5-6 minutes on each side or until the chicken juices run clear. Stir the cornstarch mixture and add to the pan. Add peas, broth, mushrooms and the celery mixture. Bring to a boil; cook and stir for 2 minutes or until thickened. Stir in cashews; serve with rice.

**NUTRITION FACTS** 1 chicken breast half equals 573 cal., 26 g fat (4 g sat. fat), 63 mg chol., 1425 mg sodium, 48 g carb. (8 g sugars, 6 g fiber), 36 g pro.

EAT SMART

# Parmesan Crust Chicken

For this dish, I coat the chicken in a light crumb coating with a mild Parmesan flavor. I don't know where I got the recipe, but it's something a little different...and so easy to multiply when we have guests.
—**LISA FRANCIS** ELBA, AL

**PREP:** 10 MIN. • **BAKE:** 45 MIN.
**MAKES:** 2 SERVINGS

- 3  tablespoons dry bread crumbs
- 2  tablespoons grated Parmesan cheese
- 1  tablespoon minced fresh parsley or 1 teaspoon dried parsley flakes
- 1  teaspoon dried oregano
- ¼  teaspoon salt
- ¼  teaspoon paprika
- ¼  teaspoon pepper
- 2  bone-in chicken breast halves (8 ounces each)
- 1  tablespoon butter, melted

In a shallow dish, combine the first seven ingredients. Brush the chicken with butter, then coat with the crumb mixture. Place in an 11x7-in. baking dish coated with cooking spray. Bake, uncovered, at 350° for 45-50 minutes or until a thermometer reads 170°.

**NUTRITION FACTS** 1 chicken breast equals 355 cal., 17 g fat (7 g sat. fat), 129 mg chol., 444 mg sodium, 6 g carb. (0 sugars, 1 g fiber), 42 g pro. *Diabetic Exchanges:* 5 lean meat, 1 fat, ½ starch.

# Grilled Herbed Turkey Tenderloins

I frequently serve these turkey tenderloins with grilled potatoes and rosemary or grilled summer vegetables. A marinade of fragrant herbs and soy sauce creates a lovely flavor combination.

—**PAMELA ANDERSON** NOBLESVILLE, IN

---

**PREP:** 10 MIN. + MARINATING
**GRILL:** 15 MIN.
**MAKES:** 2 SERVINGS

---

- ¼  cup canola oil
- ¼  cup reduced-sodium soy sauce
- ½  teaspoon dried basil
- ½  teaspoon dried marjoram
- ½  teaspoon dried thyme
- 2  turkey breast tenderloins (6 ounces each)

**1.** In a small bowl, combine canola oil, soy sauce, basil, marjoram and thyme. Pour ⅓ cup into a large resealable plastic bag; add turkey. Seal bag and turn to coat; refrigerate for up to 4 hours. Cover and refrigerate the remaining marinade for basting.

**2.** Drain and discard the marinade from the turkey. Using long-handled tongs, moisten a paper towel with cooking oil and use it to lightly coat the grill rack.

**3.** Grill the turkey, covered, over medium heat or broil 4 in. from the heat for 12-14 minutes or until a meat thermometer reads 170°, turning twice and basting occasionally with reserved marinade.

**NUTRITION FACTS** 1 serving equals 341 cal., 19 g fat (2 g sat. fat), 83 mg chol., 817 mg sodium, 1 g carb. (0 sugars, 0 fiber), 41 g pro.

**EAT SMART FAST FIX**

# Sassy Chicken & Peppers

This quick chicken dinner tastes like a naked taco and is bursting with fresh flavors. It can all be prepared in one pan for easy cleanup.

**—DORIS HEATH** FRANKLIN, NC

**START TO FINISH:** 25 MIN.
**MAKES:** 2 SERVINGS

- 2  boneless skinless chicken breast halves (4 ounces each)
- 2  teaspoons taco seasoning
- 4  teaspoons canola oil, divided
- 1  small onion, halved and sliced
- ½  small green bell pepper, julienned
- ½  small sweet red pepper, julienned
- ¼  cup salsa
- 1  tablespoon lime juice

**1.** Sprinkle chicken with seasoning. In a small nonstick skillet, cook the chicken in 2 teaspoons oil over medium heat for 4-5 minutes on each side or until the juices run clear. Remove the chicken from the pan and keep warm.

**2.** Saute onion and peppers in the remaining oil until crisp-tender; stir in salsa and lime juice. Spoon the mixture over the chicken.

**NUTRITION FACTS** 1 serving equals 239 cal., 12 g fat (1 g sat. fat), 63 mg chol., 377 mg sodium, 8 g carb. (4 g sugars, 1 g fiber), 24 g pro. *Diabetic Exchanges:* 3 lean meat, 2 fat, 1 vegetable.

# Chicken Paella

Turmeric lends flavor as well as a pretty golden color to this Spanish-style entree. Haven't tried Arborio rice? You'll love its creamy texture.

—*TASTE OF HOME* **TEST KITCHEN**

**PREP:** 10 MIN. • **COOK:** 45 MIN.
**MAKES:** 2 SERVINGS

- 2 boneless skinless chicken thighs (about ½ pound), cut into chunks
- ½ cup cubed fully cooked ham
- ⅓ cup chopped onion
- ⅓ cup julienned sweet red pepper
- 1 tablespoon olive oil, divided
- ½ cup uncooked arborio rice
- ½ teaspoon ground turmeric
- ½ teaspoon ground cumin
- ½ teaspoon minced garlic
- ⅛ teaspoon salt
- 1 cup plus 2 tablespoons chicken broth
- ¾ cup frozen peas, thawed

**1.** In a large skillet, saute chicken, ham, onion and red pepper in 2 teaspoons oil until the chicken is browned on all sides. Remove with a slotted spoon.

**2.** In the same skillet, saute rice in the remaining oil until lightly browned. Stir in turmeric, cumin, garlic and salt. Return the meat and vegetables to the pan; toss lightly. Add broth; bring to a boil. Reduce heat to medium; cover and simmer for 30-35 minutes or until the rice is tender. Stir in peas.

**NUTRITION FACTS** 1 serving equals 490 cal., 17 g fat (4 g sat. fat), 75 mg chol., 1027 mg sodium, 53 g carb. (6 g sugars, 4 g fiber), 31 g pro.

**DID YOU KNOW?**

Paella is a traditional Spanish dish and open to experimentation—you can add shrimp or other seafood if you like, or spicy sausage. Turmeric gives this dish a great flavor and the customary golden color of a traditional paella. The customary spice, saffron, is very pricey.

# Chicken Chili Enchiladas

These hearty Southwestern enchiladas turn an ordinary meal into a fiesta!
—**DOROTHY PRITCHETT** WILLS POINT, TX

**PREP:** 20 MIN. • **BAKE:** 20 MIN.
**MAKES:** 2 SERVINGS

1   medium onion, thinly sliced
1   tablespoon butter
1   package (3 ounces) cream cheese, cubed
2   tablespoons canned chopped green chilies
1/8 teaspoon salt
4   flour tortillas (8 inches)
2   tablespoons canola oil
3/4 cup shredded cooked chicken
1   tablespoon 2% milk
1   cup (4 ounces) shredded Monterey Jack cheese
    Chopped green onions and sliced ripe olives, optional

**1.** In a small skillet, saute onion in butter until tender. Remove from the heat. Stir in cream cheese, chilies and salt until blended.

**2.** In another skillet, cook tortillas in oil over medium heat until warmed and lightly browned on both sides. Drain on paper towels. Spoon 1/4 of the cream cheese mixture down the center of each tortilla. Sprinkle with chicken. Roll up each tortilla and place seam side down in an 8-in. square baking dish coated with cooking spray.

**3.** Bake tortillas, uncovered, at 350° for 15 minutes. Brush tops with milk; sprinkle with cheese. Bake 5-10 minutes longer or until the cheese is melted. Sprinkle with green onions and olives if desired.

**NUTRITION FACTS** 2 enchiladas equals 877 cal., 52 g fat (23 g sat. fat), 145 mg chol., 1261 mg sodium, 61 g carb. (6 g sugars, 2 g fiber), 44 g pro.

## Turkey & Bow Ties

The scent of this sizzling skillet will get your mouth watering! It won't keep you hovering over the stove all night, either.

**—MARY RELYEA** CANASTOTA, NY

**START TO FINISH:** 30 MIN.
**MAKES:** 2 SERVINGS

1¼ cups uncooked bow tie pasta
 6 ounces turkey breast tenderloin, cut into 1-inch cubes
 2 teaspoons olive oil
 1 cup fresh broccoli florets
 1 garlic clove, minced
 ¾ cup canned Italian diced tomatoes
 ⅓ cup reduced-sodium chicken broth
 2 tablespoons white wine or additional reduced-sodium chicken broth
 ½ teaspoon dried basil
  Dash cayenne pepper
 2 tablespoons grated Parmesan cheese

**1.** Cook pasta according to package directions. Meanwhile, in a large skillet, cook turkey in oil over medium heat until the meat is no longer pink. Add broccoli and garlic; cook until broccoli is tender.

**2.** Stir in tomatoes, broth, wine, basil and cayenne. Bring to a boil. Reduce heat; simmer, uncovered, for 5-8 minutes or until heated through, stirring occasionally. Drain the pasta; add to the turkey mixture and toss to coat. Sprinkle with cheese.

**NUTRITION FACTS** 1¼ cups equals 380 cal., 8 g fat (2 g sat. fat), 46 mg chol., 583 mg sodium, 45 g carb. (8 g sugars, 3 g fiber), 30 g pro. *Diabetic Exchanges:* 3 lean meat, 2½ starch, 1 vegetable, 1 fat.

**⑤INGREDIENTS FAST FIX▶**

# Chicken with Rosemary Butter Sauce

It doesn't require a ton of effort to plate this rich and creamy chicken entree. Give it a try!

**—CONNIE MCDOWELL** GREENWOOD, DE

**START TO FINISH:** 20 MIN.
**MAKES:** 2 SERVINGS

2   boneless skinless chicken breast halves
     (4 ounces each)
2   tablespoons butter, divided
¼   cup white wine or chicken broth
¼   cup heavy whipping cream
1½ teaspoons minced fresh rosemary

**1.** In a small skillet over medium heat, cook chicken in 1 tablespoon butter for 4-5 minutes on each side or until a thermometer reads 170°. Remove and keep warm.

**2.** Add wine to the pan; cook over medium-low heat, stirring to loosen browned bits from pan. Add cream and bring to a boil. Reduce heat; cook and stir until slightly thickened. Stir in rosemary and the remaining butter until blended. Serve with the chicken.

**NUTRITION FACTS** 1 chicken breast half with 3 tablespoons sauce equals 351 cal., 25 g fat (15 g sat. fat), 134 mg chol., 148 mg sodium, 2 g carb. (0 sugars, 0 fiber), 24 g pro.

# Santa Fe Chicken Pita Pizzas

This recipe is quick and easy, and because these are individual pizzas, they can be customized to suit each person's taste.

**—ATHENA RUSSELL** GREENVILLE, SC

---

**START TO FINISH:** 20 MIN.
**MAKES:** 2 SERVINGS

---

  2  pita breads (6 inches)
 ¼  cup refried black beans
 ¼  cup salsa
 ½  cup cubed cooked chicken breast
  1  tablespoon chopped green chilies
  1  tablespoon sliced ripe olives
 ⅓  cup shredded Colby-Monterey Jack cheese
 ¼  cup reduced-fat sour cream
  1  green onion, chopped

**1.** Place pita breads on an ungreased baking sheet; spread refried beans on top. Top with salsa, chicken, chilies, olives and cheese.

**2.** Bake at 350° for 8-10 minutes or until cheese is melted. Serve with sour cream; sprinkle with onion.

**NUTRITION FACTS** 1 pizza equals 373 cal., 10 g fat (6 g sat. fat), 54 mg chol., 762 mg sodium, 44 g carb. (4 g sugars, 3 g fiber), 24 g pro. *Diabetic Exchanges:* 3 starch, 2 lean meat, 1 fat.

FAST FIX ▶

# Chicken 'n' Sweet Potato Stew

Spice up your dinnertime fare with this Malaysian-inspired stew. Served on a bed of couscous, this dish is as good as it gets.

—**AGNES WARD** STRATFORD, ON

**START TO FINISH:** 30 MIN.
**MAKES:** 2 SERVINGS

- ⅔ pound boneless skinless chicken breasts, cut into 1-inch cubes
- ½ teaspoon minced fresh gingerroot
- 1 garlic clove, minced
- ½ teaspoon olive oil
- ½ cup chopped onion
- ½ cup chopped sweet red pepper
- ½ teaspoon ground coriander
- ½ teaspoon ground cumin
- ½ teaspoon curry powder
  Dash ground cinnamon
- 1½ cups cubed peeled sweet potatoes
- ¾ cup reduced-sodium chicken broth
- 1 cup water
- 1 tablespoon thawed orange juice concentrate
- ½ cup uncooked couscous
- 1 tablespoon cornstarch
- 6 tablespoons light coconut milk
- 1 tablespoon minced fresh cilantro

**1.** In a large skillet, saute chicken, ginger and garlic in oil until the chicken juices run clear. Add onion, pepper and seasonings; saute 4-5 minutes longer. Add sweet potatoes and broth. Bring to a boil. Reduce heat; cover and simmer for 10-12 minutes or until tender.

**2.** Meanwhile, in a small saucepan, bring water and orange juice concentrate to a boil. Stir in couscous. Cover and remove from the heat; let stand for 5-10 minutes or until water is absorbed. Fluff with a fork.

**3.** Combine cornstarch and coconut milk until smooth. Stir into the chicken mixture. Bring to a boil; cook and stir for 2 minutes or until thickened. Stir in cilantro. Serve with the couscous.

**NUTRITION FACTS** 1½ cups chicken mixture with 1 cup couscous equals 578 cal., 12 g fat (6 g sat. fat), 84 mg chol., 345 mg sodium, 75 g carb. (15 g sugars, 7 g fiber), 41 g pro.

# Chicken Reuben Roll-Ups

My Nebraskan-native husband loves Reuben sandwiches and anything chicken, so I combined his two favorites in a fun roll-up.
—**ASHLI KOTTWITZ** HERMITAGE, TN

**START TO FINISH:** 30 MINUTES
**MAKES:** 2 SERVINGS

- 2 slices swirled rye and pumpernickel bread
- 2 boneless skinless chicken breast halves (4 ounces each)
- 1/4 teaspoon garlic salt
- 1/4 teaspoon pepper
- 2 slices Swiss cheese
- 2 slices deli corned beef
- 2 tablespoons Thousand Island salad dressing
  Additional Thousand Island salad dressing, optional

**1.** Preheat oven to 425°. Tear bread into 2-in. pieces; place in a blender. Cover and pulse to form coarse crumbs; transfer to a shallow bowl.

**2.** Pound chicken breasts with a meat mallet to 1/4-in. thickness; sprinkle with garlic salt and pepper. Top with cheese and corned beef. Roll up chicken from a short side; secure with toothpicks. Brush outsides with dressing; roll in bread crumbs.

**3.** Place roll-ups on a greased baking sheet, seam side down. Bake 20-25 minutes or until chicken is no longer pink. Discard toothpicks; if desired, serve with additional dressing. A traditional Reuben sandwich can be upwards of 700 calories, 40 g fat and nearly 3,000 mg sodium! This roll-up has all the flavor without the obligatory post-dinner workout.

**NUTRITION FACTS** 1 roll-up (calculated without additional dressing) equals 326 calories, 13 g fat (4 g saturated fat), 89 mg cholesterol, 790 mg sodium, 18 g carbohydrate (3 g sugars, 2 g fiber), 32 g protein.

## EAT SMART

# Chicken Mexican Manicotti

A creative spin on traditional manicotti, this dish is packed with authentic Mexican flavor that will leave you wanting seconds.

**—LARRY PHILLIPS** SHREVEPORT, LA

**PREP:** 25 MIN. • **BAKE:** 25 MIN.
**MAKES:** 2 SERVINGS

| | |
|---|---|
| 4 | uncooked manicotti shells |
| 1 | cup cubed cooked chicken breast |
| 1 | cup salsa, divided |
| ½ | cup reduced-fat ricotta cheese |
| 2 | tablespoons sliced ripe olives |
| 4 | teaspoons minced fresh parsley |
| 1 | tablespoon diced pimientos |
| 1 | green onion, thinly sliced |
| 1 | small garlic clove, minced |
| ¼ | to ½ teaspoon hot pepper sauce |
| ⅓ | cup shredded reduced-fat Monterey Jack cheese or reduced-fat Mexican cheese blend |

**1.** Cook manicotti according to package directions. In a small bowl, combine chicken, ¼ cup salsa, ricotta cheese, olives, parsley, pimientos, green onion, garlic and hot pepper sauce. Drain the manicotti and fill with the chicken mixture.

**2.** Spread ¼ cup salsa in an 8-in. square baking dish coated with cooking spray. Top with the filled manicotti shells and remaining salsa.

**3.** Cover and bake at 400° for 20 minutes. Uncover; sprinkle with Monterey Jack cheese and bake 5-10 minutes longer or until the cheese is melted and the filling is heated through.

**NUTRITION FACTS** 1 serving equals 390 cal., 10 g fat (4 g sat. fat), 81 mg chol., 783 mg sodium, 38 g carb. (9 g sugars, 2 g fiber), 35 g pro. *Diabetic Exchanges:* 4 lean meat, 2 starch, 1 vegetable.

## TOP TIP

A rubber-tipped baby spoon makes quick work of filling manicotti pasta shells. The spoon fits nicely inside the noodle, and the filling mixture doesn't stick to its rubber coating.
**—TONI B.** KENOSHA, WI

**Pepperoni Lasagna Roll-Ups, p.220**

# Pork for Two

Casseroles and chops, roasts and ribs—here's a great collection of recipes that will put pork on your dinner table in just the right portions!

**Tender 'n' Tangy Ribs, p. 203**

**Pork with Apple-Cream Sauce, p. 212**

**Pork Chops with Herb Pesto, p. 207**

# Honey Dijon Pork

I'm fond of honey mustard salad dressing, so I duplicated that taste with this quick and easy pork recipe.
—**AUDREY THIBODEAU** GILBERT, AZ

**PREP:** 15 MIN. • **BAKE:** 50 MIN.
**MAKES:** 2 SERVINGS

2 boneless pork loin chops
(½ inch thick)
¼ teaspoon salt
Dash pepper
1 tablespoon all-purpose flour
½ cup orange juice, divided
½ cup honey
1 tablespoon Dijon mustard
¼ teaspoon dried basil
2 medium carrots, cut into
1-inch pieces
1 small onion, cut into eighths
½ small green pepper, chopped
½ small sweet red pepper, chopped

1. Sprinkle pork chops with salt and pepper; place in a heavy ovenproof skillet. In a small bowl, whisk flour and 2 tablespoons orange juice until smooth; whisk in honey, mustard, basil and the remaining orange juice. Pour over chops. Place carrots and onion around chops.

2. Cover and bake at 350° for 30 minutes. Add peppers; cover and bake 20 minutes longer or until the vegetables are tender and the pork is no longer pink.

**NUTRITION FACTS** 1 serving equals 586 cal., 11 g fat (4 g sat. fat), 82 mg chol., 558 mg sodium, 92 g carb. (79 g sugars, 4 g fiber), 35 g pro.

**TOP TIP**

Put a sweet potato in the oven to bake at the same time as the pork chops, and you'll have a complete meal for two! To bake the potato, just pierce the skin with a fork and put it in the oven at 350° for 40-45 minutes until tender.

# Tender 'n' Tangy Ribs

These ribs are so simple to prepare. Serve them at noon—
or let them simmer all day for fall-off-the-bone tenderness.
—**DENISE HATHAWAY VALASEK** PERRYSBURG, OH

**PREP:** 15 MIN. • **COOK:** 4 HOURS
**MAKES:** 2-3 SERVINGS

¾  to 1 cup white vinegar
½  cup ketchup
2  tablespoons sugar
2  tablespoons Worcestershire sauce
1  garlic clove, minced
1  teaspoon ground mustard
1  teaspoon paprika
½  to 1 teaspoon salt
⅛  teaspoon pepper
2  pounds pork spareribs
1  tablespoon canola oil

Combine the first nine ingredients in a 3-qt. slow cooker.
Cut ribs into serving-size pieces; brown in a skillet in oil.
Transfer to slow cooker. Cover and cook on low for
4-6 hours or until tender.

**NUTRITION FACTS** 1 cup equals 689 cal., 48 g fat (16 g sat.
fat), 170 mg chol., 1110 mg sodium, 22 g carb. (13 g sugars,
1 g fiber), 42 g pro.

EAT SMART **FAST FIX**

# Pork with Curried Apple & Couscous

The aroma of this delicious dinner will really whet your appetite. Curry brings earthy flavor while raisins and apples lend a touch of sweetness.

**—TASTE OF HOME TEST KITCHEN**

**START TO FINISH:** 30 MIN.
**MAKES:** 2 SERVINGS

- ¾ pound pork tenderloin
- ¼ teaspoon salt
- ⅛ teaspoon pepper
- 3 teaspoons reduced-fat butter, divided
- 1 green onion, thinly sliced
- 1 garlic clove, minced
- 1 small apple, peeled and sliced
- 1 tablespoon raisins
- 1 teaspoon cornstarch
- 1 teaspoon curry powder
- ⅓ cup reduced-sodium chicken broth
- 1½ cups hot cooked couscous

**1.** Sprinkle pork loin with salt and pepper. In a large skillet, brown the pork in 2 teaspoons butter. Reduce heat to low; cover and cook for 15-20 minutes or until a thermometer reaches 160°, turning occasionally. Remove the pork from the skillet and keep warm.

**2.** Saute onion and garlic in the remaining butter until tender. Add the apple and raisins; saute 2 minutes longer. Combine cornstarch, curry powder and broth until smooth; stir into the apple mixture. Bring to a boil; cook and stir for 1-2 minutes or until thickened. Serve with tenderloin and couscous.

**NUTRITION FACTS** 1 serving (includes ½ cup apple mixture and ¾ cup of couscous) equals 406 cal., 9 g fat (4 g sat. fat), 102 mg chol., 513 mg sodium, 41 g carb. (8 g sugars, 3 g fiber), 39 g pro. *Diabetic Exchanges:* 5 lean meat, 2 starch, 1 fat, ½ fruit.

## Pork Chops with Herb Pesto

You won't believe how much a handful of fresh garden herbs can enhance the flavor of ordinary pork chops. These would be fantastic with garlic mashed potatoes.
—**LISA BYNUM** BRANDON, MS

---

**PREP:** 15 MIN. + MARINATING • **GRILL:** 10 MIN.
**MAKES:** 2 SERVINGS

---

- 2 bone-in pork loin chops (¾ inch thick and 7 ounces each)
- ⅛ teaspoon salt
  Dash pepper
- 1 tablespoon water
- 1½ teaspoons each minced fresh rosemary, sage, thyme, parsley and basil
- 1½ teaspoons olive oil
- 1 garlic clove, minced

**1.** Sprinkle pork with salt and pepper. In a small bowl, combine water, herbs, oil and garlic; brush over both sides of the pork chops. Cover and refrigerate for at least 1 hour.

**2.** On a greased grill rack, grill the chops, covered, over medium heat or broil 4-5 in. from the heat for 4-5 minutes on each side or until a thermometer reads 145°. Let stand for 5 minutes before serving.

**NUTRITION FACTS** 1 serving equals 240 cal., 12 g fat (4 g sat. fat), 86 mg chol., 211 mg sodium, 1 g carb. (0 sugars, 0 fiber), 30 g pro. *Diabetic Exchanges:* 4 lean meat, 1 fat.

# Creamy Ham & Potatoes

If you love scalloped potatoes but have a small household, this downsized version with tender chunks of ham is just for you. Best of all, it simmers on its own in the slow cooker!

**—WENDY ROWLEY** GREEN RIVER, WY

---

**PREP:** 20 MIN. • **COOK:** 5 HOURS
**MAKES:** 2 SERVINGS

---

  2  large red potatoes, cubed
  1/3  cup cubed process cheese (Velveeta)
  3/4  cup cubed fully cooked ham
  1  tablespoon dried minced onion
  2/3  cup condensed cream of celery soup, undiluted
  2/3  cup 2% milk
  1  tablespoon all-purpose flour
  1/4  teaspoon pepper

**1.** In a greased 1½-qt. slow cooker, layer the potatoes, cheese, ham and onion.

**2.** In a small bowl, combine soup and milk; whisk in flour and pepper. Pour over potatoes. Cover and cook on low for 5-6 hours or until potatoes are tender. Stir before serving.

**NUTRITION FACTS** 1½ cups equals 398 cal., 15 g fat (6 g sat. fat), 52 mg chol., 1534 mg sodium, 45 g carb. (8 g sugars, 4 g fiber), 20 g pro.

## Favorite Italian Casserole

We usually add toasted garlic bread and a tossed salad to this hearty pizza-flavored dish to round out the meal.

**—LEE SAUERS** MIFFLINBURG, PA

**PREP:** 25 MIN. • **BAKE:** 30 MIN.
**MAKES:** 3 SERVINGS

- 3 ounces uncooked spaghetti
- 1 Italian sausage link, casing removed
- 1 small onion, sliced
- 1 small zucchini, sliced
  Dash pepper
- 1 bacon strip, cooked and crumbled
- 1/4 cup shredded Parmesan cheese
- 1 cup spaghetti sauce, divided
- 2 tablespoons chopped sweet red pepper
- 1/2 cup shredded part-skim mozzarella cheese
- 12 slices pepperoni
  Dash each dried oregano, thyme and basil

**1.** Cook spaghetti according to package directions. Meanwhile, crumble sausage into a small skillet; add onion. Cook over medium heat until the meat is no longer pink; drain.

**2.** Drain the spaghetti. Arrange zucchini in a shallow 1-qt. baking dish coated with cooking spray; sprinkle with pepper. Layer with bacon, Parmesan cheese, 1/2 cup spaghetti sauce, the spaghetti, the remaining sauce, red pepper, the sausage mixture, mozzarella cheese and pepperoni.

**3.** Sprinkle with herbs. Bake, uncovered, at 350° for 30-35 minutes or until the vegetables are tender.

**NUTRITION FACTS** 1 serving equals 356 cal., 14 g fat (6 g sat. fat), 48 mg chol., 1018 mg sodium, 35 g carb. (9 g sugars, 3 g fiber), 23 g pro.

EAT SMART

# Pork with Apple-Cream Sauce

This savory, satisfying meal is simple enough for a weeknight and elegant enough for company or a Sunday dinner.

—**MARGARET LOWENBERG** KINGMAN, AZ

**PREP:** 10 MIN. • **COOK:** 30 MIN.
**MAKES:** 2 SERVINGS

- 1 pork tenderloin (¾ pound)
- ½ teaspoon dried thyme
- 3 teaspoons butter, divided
- ¼ cup finely chopped red onion
- 1 large apple, peeled and thinly sliced
- 2 tablespoons apple juice or apple brandy, divided
- ¼ cup white wine or reduced-sodium chicken broth
- ½ cup reduced-sodium chicken broth
- 1 teaspoon cornstarch
- ¼ teaspoon salt
- ⅛ teaspoon pepper
- ⅓ cup half-and-half cream
- 1 tablespoon Dijon mustard

1. Rub pork loin with thyme. In a large skillet, brown the pork in 1½ teaspoons butter; remove and set aside. In the same skillet, saute onion in the remaining butter until tender. Stir in apple; cook and stir for 2 minutes. Add 1½ teaspoons apple juice or brandy; cook and stir 30 seconds longer. Transfer to a bowl.

2. Add wine or broth and the remaining apple juice or brandy to the skillet. Bring to a boil over medium heat; cook 5 minutes or until the liquid is reduced by half. Stir in broth, pork and apple mixture. Bring to a boil. Reduce heat; simmer, uncovered, for 20 minutes or until a thermometer reads 160°, turning the pork occasionally. Remove the pork from the skillet and keep warm.

3. In a small bowl, combine cornstarch, salt and pepper; gradually stir in cream and mustard. Stir into the apple mixture. Bring to a boil; cook and stir for 2 minutes or until thickened. Serve with the pork.

**NUTRITION FACTS** 1 serving equals 400 cal., 16 g fat (8 g sat. fat), 130 mg chol., 903 mg sodium, 19 g carb. (14 g sugars, 2 g fiber), 37 g pro. *Diabetic Exchanges:* 5 lean meat, 1 vegetable, 1 fruit, 1 fat.

# Ham and Broccoli Linguine

Thyme provides an earthy flavor to this hearty pasta dish. This simple meal in one can be on your dinner table tonight!
—*TASTE OF HOME* TEST KITCHEN

---

**START TO FINISH:** 30 MIN.
**MAKES:** 2 SERVINGS

---

 3   ounces uncooked linguine
 1   cup fresh broccoli florets
½   cup fresh cauliflowerets
 1   small carrot, chopped
½   cup sliced fresh mushrooms
 1   tablespoon butter
 1   tablespoon all-purpose flour
¼   teaspoon dried thyme
⅛   teaspoon salt
⅛   teaspoon pepper
¾   cup 2% milk
¾   cup shredded cheddar cheese
 1   cup julienned fully cooked ham

**1.** In a large saucepan, cook linguine according to package directions. Add broccoli, cauliflower and carrot during the last 5 minutes of cooking.

**2.** Meanwhile, in another saucepan, saute mushrooms in butter until tender. Stir in flour, thyme, salt and pepper until blended; gradually add milk. Bring to a boil; cook and stir for 2 minutes or until thickened. Stir in cheese.

**3.** Drain the linguine and vegetables; transfer to a serving bowl. Add the ham and sauce mixture; toss to coat.

**NUTRITION FACTS** 2½ cups equals 502 cal., 21 g fat (11 g sat. fat), 81 mg chol., 1443 mg sodium, 48 g carb. (10 g sugars, 4 g fiber), 35 g pro.

EAT SMART

# Gingered Pork and Veggies

I rely on this savory dish when time is short. It's wonderful served with a combination of brown and white rice.
—**DOROTHY BATEMAN** CARVER, MA

**PREP:** 20 MIN. • **COOK:** 30 MIN.
**MAKES:** 2 SERVINGS

- 2 tablespoons all-purpose flour
- ¾ pound pork chop suey meat or cubed pork tenderloin
- 1 tablespoon canola oil
- ½ cup water
- 1 teaspoon lemon juice
- ¼ teaspoon sugar
- ¼ to ½ teaspoon ground ginger
- ¼ teaspoon garlic powder
- ¼ teaspoon chicken bouillon granules
- ⅛ teaspoon pepper
- 1 small onion, sliced
- ½ medium green pepper, sliced
- ¼ cup sliced celery
- 2 tablespoons chopped sweet red pepper
- 1½ teaspoons cornstarch
- 1 tablespoon cold water
  Hot cooked rice, optional

1. Place flour in a large resealable plastic bag; add pork and shake to coat. In a large skillet, brown the pork in the oil over medium heat; drain.

2. In a small bowl, combine water, lemon juice, sugar, ground ginger, garlic powder, bouillon and pepper; pour over the pork. Add onion, green pepper, celery and red pepper; bring to a boil. Reduce heat; cover and simmer for 20 minutes.

3. Combine cornstarch and cold water until smooth; stir into the pork mixture. Bring to a boil, then cook and stir for 2 minutes or until thickened. Serve over rice if desired.

**NUTRITION FACTS** 1 cup equals 367 cal., 17 g fat (4 g sat. fat), 100 mg chol., 193 mg sodium, 15 g carb. (4 g sugars, 2 g fiber), 37 g pro. *Diabetic Exchanges:* 4 lean meat, 1½ fat, 1 starch.

**TOP TIP**

Try using arrowroot or flour instead of cornstarch as a thickener. Start with a little less arrowroot than the amount of cornstarch called for; adjust as needed. If using flour, use twice as much all-purpose flour as the amount of cornstarch called for. Mix either with liquid to make a slurry before heating.

# Kielbasa with Curried Rice

This refreshingly different dish has been a favorite of our children for years. Recently, I multiplied the recipe several times and served it at a family reunion. Not a drop was left over!
—**CARMA BLOSSER** LIVERMORE, CO

**START TO FINISH:** 25 MIN.
**MAKES:** 2 SERVINGS

- ½ pound smoked kielbasa, cut into ½-inch slices
- ¾ cup fresh or frozen snow peas, thawed
- ⅓ cup chopped green pepper
- ¼ cup chopped onion
- 2 teaspoons curry powder
- 2 tablespoons butter
- 1 cup cooked instant rice
- ⅔ cup water
- ⅔ cup condensed cream of chicken soup, undiluted
- ½ cup canned diced tomatoes

In a large skillet, saute the kielbasa, snow peas, green pepper, onion and curry powder in butter until vegetables are tender. Stir in the remaining ingredients; heat through.

**NUTRITION FACTS** 2 cups equals 426 cal., 18 g fat (7 g sat. fat), 93 mg chol., 1877 mg sodium, 43 g carb. (9 g sugars, 5 g fiber), 25 g pro.

# Pepperoni Lasagna Roll-Ups

My husband is in the military, and when he is away from home it's hard to come up with meals just for myself. I combined some leftover ingredients from making lasagna to come up with this recipe.

**—JENNIFER JUDAY** COPPERAS COVE, TX

**PREP:** 25 MIN. • **BAKE:** 25 MIN.
**MAKES:** 3 SERVINGS

- 3  lasagna noodles
- ¾  cup ricotta cheese
- ½  teaspoon minced chives
- ½  teaspoon dried oregano
- ½  teaspoon dried basil
- 24  slices pepperoni
- 3  slices Swiss cheese, cut into thirds
- 1  cup meatless spaghetti sauce
- ¼  cup shredded Parmesan cheese

**1.** Cook noodles according to package directions; drain. Combine ricotta cheese, chives, oregano and basil; spread ¼ cup over each noodle to within ½ in. of edges. Top with pepperoni and Swiss cheese; carefully roll up.

**2.** Place rolls seam side down in a greased shallow 1-qt. baking dish; top with spaghetti sauce. Cover and bake at 350° for 20-25 minutes or until bubbly.

**3.** Sprinkle with Parmesan cheese. Let stand for 5 minutes before serving.

**NUTRITION FACTS** 1 roll-up equals 410 cal., 22 g fat (13 g sat. fat), 68 mg chol., 894 mg sodium, 30 g carb. (10 g sugars, 2 g fiber), 23 g pro.

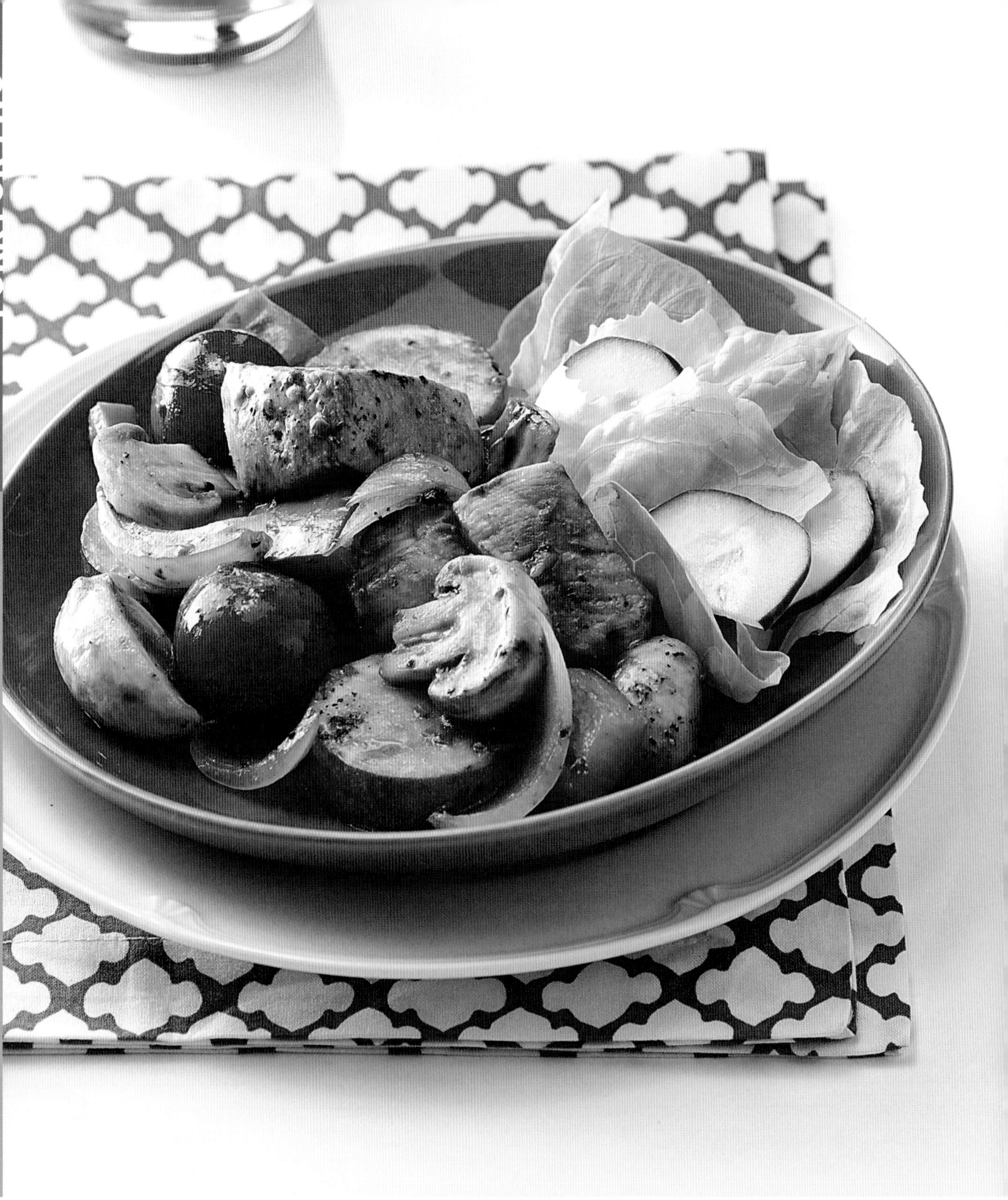

## Skewerless Stovetop Kabobs

We love this quick and easy recipe. It's also great as traditional kabobs, threaded onto skewers and cooked on the grill.

**—JENNIFER MITCHELL** ALTOONA, PA

---

**START TO FINISH:** 25 MIN.
**MAKES:** 2 SERVINGS

---

- ½ pound pork tenderloin, cut into ¾-inch cubes
- 6 tablespoons fat-free Italian salad dressing, divided
- 1 large green pepper, cut into ¾-inch pieces
- 1 small zucchini, cut into ½-inch slices
- ¼ pound medium fresh mushrooms, halved
- ½ large sweet onion, cut into wedges
- ½ cup cherry tomatoes
- ⅛ teaspoon pepper
  Dash seasoned salt

**1.** In a large nonstick skillet, saute pork in 2 tablespoons salad dressing until the meat is no longer pink. Remove pork from the skillet and keep warm.

**2.** Cook pepper, zucchini, mushrooms, onion, tomatoes, pepper and seasoned salt in the remaining salad dressing until the vegetables are tender. Return the pork to the skillet; heat through.

**NUTRITION FACTS** 2 cup equals 236 cal., 5 g fat (2 g sat. fat), 65 mg chol., 757 mg sodium, 22 g carb. (12 g sugars, 4 g fiber), 27 g pro. *Diabetic Exchanges:* 3 lean meat, 2 starch.

## Tuscan Pork Medallions

Prosciutto, tomatoes and herbs add delightful Italian flavor to pork tenderloin. The aroma is divine as the rich and creamy sauce cooks.

—**LORRAINE CALAND** SHUNIAH, ON

**START TO FINISH:** 30 MIN.
**MAKES:** 2 SERVINGS

| | |
|---|---|
| ¾ | pound pork tenderloin, cut into 1-inch slices |
| ¼ | teaspoon salt |
| ⅛ | teaspoon pepper |
| 1 | tablespoon butter |
| 2 | thin slices prosciutto or deli ham, chopped |
| 2 | garlic cloves, minced |
| 1½ | teaspoons minced fresh sage or ½ teaspoon dried sage leaves |
| 2 | tablespoons balsamic vinegar |
| ½ | cup heavy whipping cream |
| ¾ | cup chopped plum tomatoes |
| 4 | fresh basil leaves, thinly sliced |
| 1 | teaspoon grated Parmesan cheese |

**1.** Sprinkle pork with salt and pepper. In a large skillet over medium heat, cook the pork in butter until the meat reaches desired doneness (for medium-rare, a thermometer should read 145°; medium, 160°). Remove the pork from the skillet and set aside.

**2.** Saute prosciutto in the drippings until browned. Add garlic and sage; cook 1 minute longer. Add vinegar, stirring to loosen browned bits from pan.

**3.** Stir in cream; bring to a boil. Reduce heat; cook and stir for 1-2 minutes or until slightly thickened. Add the pork and tomatoes; heat through. Sprinkle each serving with basil and cheese.

**NUTRITION FACTS** 1 serving equals 514 cal., 36 g fat (20 g sat. fat), 205 mg chol., 718 mg sodium, 8 g carb. (4 g sugars, 1 g fiber), 40 g pro.

**TOP TIP**

In the winter months, when it's harder to get good fresh tomatoes, try using sun-dried tomatoes in this recipe instead. Sun-dried tomatoes have a stronger, more intense flavor than fresh, so cut back on the quantity.

**Pepper and
Salsa Cod, p. 246**

# Fish for Two

Healthy, satisfying and delicious, fish and seafood can be comforting and casual or sophisticated and elegant—and just right for a meal for two!

**Coconut-Mango Mahi Mahi, p. 249**

**Smoked Salmon Quesadillas with Creamy Chipotle Sauce, p. 238**

**Tuna Zucchini Cakes, p. 241**

# Salmon Salad with Glazed Walnuts

This main-dish salad was inspired by something I ate while on a trip. The glazed walnuts give it a little something special. I've also topped it with grilled chicken or portobello mushrooms when they're on hand.

**—JOANNA KOBERNIK** BERKLEY, MICHIGAN

**START TO FINISH:** 15 MIN. • **MAKES:** 2 SERVINGS

- 2 salmon fillets (4 ounces each)
- 6 tablespoons reduced-fat balsamic vinaigrette, divided
- 1/8 teaspoon pepper
- 4 cups spring mix salad greens
- 1/4 cup glazed walnuts
- 2 tablespoons crumbled blue cheese

**1.** Brush salmon with 2 tablespoons vinaigrette, then sprinkle with pepper. On a greased grill rack, cook the salmon, covered, over medium heat or broil 4 in. from heat 3-4 minutes on each side or just until fish begins to flake easily with a fork.

**2.** In a bowl, toss salad greens with the remaining vinaigrette. Divide between two plates; sprinkle with walnuts and cheese. Top each with a salmon fillet.

**NUTRITION FACTS** 1 serving equals 374 calories, 25g fat (5 g saturated fat), 64 mg cholesterol, 607 mg sodium, 13g carbohydrate (8 g sugars, 4 g fiber), 24 g protein. *Diabetic Exchanges:* 3 lean meat, 3 fat, 1/2 starch.

# Comforting Tuna Casserole

My mother gave me the recipe for this classic casserole 20 years ago. Sometimes I use sliced stuffed olives instead of pimientos.
—**DOROTHY COLEMAN** HOBE SOUND, FL

**PREP:** 15 MIN. • **BAKE:** 20 MIN.
**MAKES:** 2 SERVINGS

1¾ cups uncooked wide egg noodles
6 teaspoons reduced-fat butter, divided
4 teaspoons all-purpose flour
¼ teaspoon salt
  Dash pepper
¾ cup 2% milk
3 ounces reduced-fat cream cheese
1 pouch (2½ ounces) albacore white tuna in water
2 tablespoons diced pimientos
2 teaspoons minced chives
2 slices Muenster cheese (¾ ounce each)
2 tablespoons soft bread crumbs

**1.** Cook noodles according to package directions. Meanwhile, in a small saucepan over medium heat, melt 5 teaspoons butter. Stir in flour, salt and pepper until blended; gradually add milk. Bring to a boil over medium heat; cook and stir for 1-2 minutes or until thickened. Reduce heat to medium-low; add cream cheese, tuna, pimientos and chives. Cook and stir until the cheese is melted.

**2.** Drain the noodles. Spread ¼ cup of the tuna mixture into a 3-cup baking dish coated with cooking spray. Layer with half the noodles, ½ cup of the tuna mixture and one slice of cheese. Repeat the layers.

**3.** Microwave the remaining butter on high, stirring every 30 seconds; stir in bread crumbs. Sprinkle over the top of the casserole. Bake, uncovered, at 350° for 20-25 minutes or until bubbly.

**NUTRITION FACTS** 1½ cup equals 493 cal., 26 g fat (15 g sat. fat), 118 mg chol., 941 mg sodium, 37 g carb. (7 g sugars, 2 g fiber), 28 g pro.

# Zippy Tomato-Topped Snapper

Seafood fans will be more than satisfied with this pleasantly zesty entree. Serve the fish with a salad and baked potato, and you've got a balanced meal.

**—MARY ANNE ZIMMERMAN** SILVER SPRINGS, FL

---

**PREP:** 10 MIN. • **BAKE:** 25 MIN.
**MAKES:** 2 SERVINGS

---

- 1 red snapper fillet (¾ pound), cut in half
- ¾ teaspoon lemon-pepper seasoning
- ⅛ teaspoon salt
- ½ cup canned diced tomatoes and green chilies
- 2 tablespoons chopped onion
- 2 tablespoons chopped celery
- 1 tablespoon minced fresh parsley
- ⅛ teaspoon celery seed

**1.** Sprinkle both sides of red snapper with lemon pepper and salt. Place in a greased 11x7-in. baking dish.

**2.** Combine tomatoes, onion, celery, parsley and celery seed; spoon over the snapper.

**3.** Cover and bake at 350° for 25-30 minutes or until the fish flakes easily with a fork.

**NUTRITION FACTS** 1 serving equals 179 cal., 2 g fat (0 sat. fat), 60 mg chol., 643 mg sodium, 4 g carb. (1 g sugars, 1 g fiber), 34 g pro. *Diabetic Exchanges:* 5 lean meat, 1 vegetable.

FAST FIX

# Tangy Crab-Stuffed Sole

There's a pleasant lemony tang to this seafood entree. Serve it with rice pilaf and asparagus.

—**JUDIE ANGLEN** RIVERTON, WY

**START TO FINISH:** 20 MIN.
**MAKES:** 2 SERVINGS

### DILL SAUCE

¼ cup butter
4½ teaspoons all-purpose flour
½ cup chicken broth
¼ teaspoon dill weed
1 to 3 teaspoons lemon juice

### FISH

1 large egg, lightly beaten
1 package (8 ounces) imitation crabmeat, flaked
¼ cup finely chopped celery
3 tablespoons dry bread crumbs
1 tablespoon grated Parmesan cheese
1 teaspoon butter, melted
2 sole or orange roughy fillets (6 ounces each)

**1.** For dill sauce, melt butter in a microwave-safe bowl; stir in flour until smooth. Stir in broth and dill until blended. Microwave, uncovered, on high for 2-3 minutes, stirring after each minute, until the sauce comes to a boil and is thickened. Stir in lemon juice; keep warm.

**2.** In a small bowl, combine the egg, crab, celery, bread crumbs, Parmesan cheese and butter. Spoon onto the center of each fillet; roll up fish around filling. Place in a 9-in. round microwave-safe dish. Cover with waxed paper.

**3.** Microwave on high for 5-6 minutes or until fish flakes easily with a fork and a thermometer inserted into stuffing reads 160°. Serve with dill sauce.

**NOTE** This recipe was tested in a 1,100-watt microwave.

**NUTRITION FACTS** 1 serving equals 500 cal., 29 g fat (17 g sat. fat), 205 mg chol., 1342 mg sodium, 28 g carb. (1 g sugars, 1 g fiber), 30 g pro.

# Weeknight Catfish Wraps

Here's an easy way to enjoy fish tacos—tuck golden brown catfish nuggets into tortillas with a quick coleslaw filling.
**—MONICA PERRY** BOISE, ID

**PREP:** 10 MIN. + CHILLING • **COOK:** 10 MIN.
**MAKES:** 2 SERVINGS

1½  cups coleslaw mix
 2  tablespoons finely chopped onion
⅛  teaspoon pepper
 1  teaspoon Creole or Cajun seasoning, divided
¼  cup coleslaw salad dressing
 2  tablespoons pancake mix
½  pound catfish fillets, cut into 2-inch pieces
 1  teaspoon canola oil
 4  flour tortillas (6 inches), warmed

**1.** In a small bowl, combine coleslaw mix, onion, pepper and ¼ teaspoon seasoning. Stir in salad dressing. Cover and refrigerate for at least 30 minutes.

**2.** In a resealable plastic bag, combine pancake mix and the remaining seasoning. Add fish; toss to coat.

**3.** In a small nonstick skillet over medium heat, cook the fish in oil until it is light golden brown on all sides and flakes easily with a fork.

**4.** Spoon the coleslaw mixture onto tortillas; top with the fish and roll up.

**NUTRITION FACTS** 2 wraps equals 469 cal., 23 g fat (3 g sat. fat), 62 mg chol., 1207 mg sodium, 39 g carb. (6 g sugars, 2 g fiber), 25 g pro.

FAST FIX ▶

# Smoked Salmon Quesadillas with Creamy Chipotle Sauce

These quesadillas taste extra-special, but take just minutes to make. A fresh burst of chopped fresh cilantro is the perfect finishing touch.

**—DANIEL SHEMTOB** IRVINE, CA

**START TO FINISH:** 25 MIN.
**MAKES:** 3 SERVINGS (⅔ CUP SAUCE)

| | |
|---|---|
| ½ | cup creme fraiche or sour cream |
| 2 | tablespoons minced chipotle peppers in adobo sauce |
| 2 | tablespoons lime juice |
| ⅛ | teaspoon salt |
| ⅛ | teaspoon pepper |

**QUESADILLAS**

| | |
|---|---|
| ¼ | cup cream cheese, softened |
| 2 | ounces fresh goat cheese |
| 3 | flour tortillas (8 inches) |
| 3 | ounces smoked salmon or lox, chopped |
| ¼ | cup finely chopped shallots |
| ¼ | cup finely chopped roasted sweet red pepper |
| | Coarsely chopped fresh cilantro |

**1.** In a small bowl, mix the first five ingredients. In another bowl, mix cream cheese and goat cheese until blended; spread over tortillas. Top half side of each with salmon, shallots and red pepper; fold over.

**2.** Place the quesadillas on a greased griddle. Cook over medium heat for 1-2 minutes on each side or until lightly browned and the cheeses are melted. Serve with the sauce; top with cilantro.

**NUTRITION FACTS** 1 quesadilla with 3 tablespoons sauce equals 453 cal., 28 g fat (16 g sat. fat), 74 mg chol., 1118 mg sodium, 33 g carb. (2 g sugars, 0 fiber), 15 g pro.

TOP TIP

Have an opened package of tortillas in the refrigerator? You can use them to make a quick, crunchy snack! Brush the tortillas with butter and then sprinkle them with herbs or cinnamon and sugar. Bake on a cookie sheet until crisp.

# Tuna Zucchini Cakes

Here's a great combination of seafood and garden vegetables. Our friends like that it's so colorful and pretty, not to mention wonderful to eat!

—**BILLIE BLANTON** KINGSPORT, TN

**START TO FINISH:** 25 MIN.
**MAKES:** 3 SERVINGS

1 tablespoon butter
½ cup finely chopped onion
1 pouch (6.4 ounces) light tuna in water
1 cup seasoned bread crumbs, divided
1 cup shredded zucchini
2 large eggs, lightly beaten
⅓ cup minced fresh parsley
1 teaspoon lemon juice
½ teaspoon salt
⅛ teaspoon pepper
2 tablespoons canola oil

**1.** In a large saucepan, heat butter over medium-high heat. Add onion; cook and stir until tender. Remove from heat.

**2.** Add tuna, ½ cup bread crumbs, zucchini, eggs, parsley, lemon juice, salt and pepper to the onion; mix lightly but thoroughly. Shape into six ½-in.-thick patties; coat with the remaining bread crumbs.

**3.** In a large skillet, heat oil over medium heat. Add tuna patties; cook 3 minutes on each side or until golden brown and heated through.

**NUTRITION FACTS** 2 tuna cakes equals 400 cal., 19 g fat (5 g sat. fat), 170 mg chol., 1261 mg sodium, 31 g carb. (4 g sugars, 3 g fiber), 26 g pro.

# Grilled Tilapia with Pineapple Salsa

Just because you're serving smaller meals doesn't mean you have to sacrifice flavor. This delicious fish dish is sure to please with its tropical flavor.

—**BETH FLEMING** DOWNERS GROVE, IL

**START TO FINISH:** 25 MIN.
**MAKES:** 2 SERVINGS (½ CUP SALSA)

½   cup cubed fresh pineapple
1   tablespoon chopped green onion
1   tablespoon finely chopped green pepper
1   tablespoon minced fresh cilantro
3   teaspoons lime juice, divided
¼   teaspoon salt, divided
     Dash cayenne pepper
1   teaspoon canola oil
2   tilapia fillets (4 ounces each)
     Dash pepper

**1.** In a small bowl, combine pineapple, green onion, green pepper, cilantro, 1 teaspoon lime juice, ⅛ teaspoon salt and the cayenne. Chill until serving.

**2.** Combine oil and the remaining lime juice; drizzle over fish fillets. Sprinkle with pepper and the remaining salt.

**3.** On a greased grill rack, grill tilapia, covered, over medium heat or broil 4 in. from the heat for 3-4 minutes on each side or until the fish flakes easily with a fork. Serve with salsa.

**NUTRITION FACTS** 1 fillet equals 137 cal., 3 g fat (1 g sat. fat), 55 mg chol., 337 mg sodium, 6 g carb. (4 g sugars, 1 g fiber), 21 g pro. *Diabetic Exchanges:* 3 lean meat, ½ fruit.

## TOP TIP

When buying frozen fish, look for fillets that are frozen solid, with no ice crystals or water stains on the package and no yellow or white discoloration on the fish itself (an indication of drying out or freezer burn). Thaw the fish in its original packaging in the refrigerator. Do not refreeze.

# Flounder with Shrimp Stuffing

For a perfect date-night meal, try this delicious stuffed flounder. You don't have to go to a fancy restaurant when you can make a recipe that is sure to impress!

**—MARIE FORTE** RARITAN, NJ

**PREP:** 30 MIN. • **BAKE:** 20 MIN.
**MAKES:** 2 SERVINGS

**STUFFING**
- 2 tablespoons butter
- 2 tablespoons finely chopped onion
- 1 tablespoon finely chopped celery
- 1 tablespoon finely chopped green pepper
- 8 uncooked medium shrimp, peeled and deveined
- 2 tablespoons beef broth
- ½ teaspoon diced pimientos, drained
- ½ teaspoon Worcestershire sauce
- ¼ teaspoon dill weed
- ¼ teaspoon minced chives
  Dash salt
  Dash cayenne pepper
- ½ cup soft bread crumbs

**FISH**
- 2 flounder fillets (3 ounces each)
- 2 tablespoons butter, melted
- 2 teaspoons lemon juice
- ½ teaspoon minced fresh parsley
  Dash paprika
  Salt and pepper to taste

**1.** In a large skillet, melt butter. Add onion, celery and green pepper; saute until tender. Add shrimp; cook and stir until the shrimp turn pink. Add broth, pimientos, Worcestershire sauce, dill, chives, salt and cayenne; heat through. Remove from the heat; stir in bread crumbs.

**2.** Spoon about ½ cup of the stuffing onto each flounder fillet; roll up. Place seam side down in a greased 9x9-in. baking dish. Drizzle with butter and lemon juice. Sprinkle with the seasonings. Bake, uncovered, at 375° for 15-20 minutes or until the fish flakes easily with a fork.

**NUTRITION FACTS** 1 serving equals 353 cal., 25 g fat (15 g sat. fat), 163 mg chol., 507 mg sodium, 8 g carb. (1 g sugars, 1 g fiber), 24 g pro.

**EAT SMART** **FAST FIX** ▶

# Pepper and Salsa Cod

After tasting a sample of a similar dish at the grocery store, my husband figured out how to make this awesome cod topped with salsa and peppers.

**—ROBYN GALLAGHER** YORKTOWN, VA

**START TO FINISH:** 30 MIN.
**MAKES:** 2 SERVINGS

- 2   cod or haddock fillets (6 ounces each)
- 1   teaspoon olive oil
- ¼   teaspoon salt
     Dash pepper
- ⅓   cup orange juice
- ¼   cup salsa
- ⅓   cup julienned green pepper
- ⅓   cup julienned sweet red pepper
     Hot cooked rice

**1.** Preheat oven to 350°. Brush both sides of fish fillets with olive oil; place in a greased 11x7-in. baking dish. Sprinkle with salt and pepper. Pour orange juice over fish; top with salsa and peppers.

**2.** Bake, covered, 17-20 minutes or until the fish just begins to flake easily with a fork. Serve with rice.

**NUTRITION FACTS** 1 fillet (calculated without rice) equals 183 cal., 3 g fat (1 g sat. fat), 65 mg chol., 512 mg sodium, 9 g carb. (6 g sugars, 1 g fiber), 27 g pro. *Diabetic Exchanges:* 4 lean meat, 1 vegetable, ½ fat.

# Coconut-Mango Mahi Mahi

An impressive, slightly sweet preparation for this popular fish.

**—DON THOMPSON** HOUSTON, OH

**START TO FINISH:** 30 MIN.
**MAKES:** 2 SERVINGS (½ CUP SAUCE)

- ¼  cup all-purpose flour
- 1  large egg, beaten
- ½  cup dry bread crumbs
- ½  cup flaked coconut
- 2  mahi mahi fillets (5 ounces each)
- 2  teaspoons peanut or canola oil
- 1  medium mango, peeled and cubed
- 2  tablespoons white wine or chicken broth
- 1  tablespoon packed brown sugar
- 1  garlic clove, halved
- 1  teaspoon finely chopped crystallized ginger
- 1  teaspoon soy sauce
- ⅛  teaspoon pepper
- 1  tablespoon minced fresh basil

**1.** Place flour and egg in separate shallow bowls. In a third shallow bowl, combine bread crumbs and coconut. Dip fillets in the flour, the egg, and then the bread crumb mixture.

**2.** In a large skillet over medium heat, cook the fillets in oil for 4-5 minutes on each side or until golden brown on the outside and the fish just turns opaque in the center.

**3.** Meanwhile, in a food processor, combine mango, wine, brown sugar, garlic, ginger, soy sauce and pepper; cover and process until blended. Stir in basil. Serve with the fish.

**NUTRITION FACTS** 1 fillet equals 487 cal., 15 g fat (7 g sat. fat), 200 mg chol., 488 mg sodium, 54 g carb. (30 g sugars, 4 g fiber), 34 g pro.

# Crumb-Topped Baked Fish

Flaky and mild white fish is treated to a tasty coating of bread crumbs, cheese and seasonings in this savory entree.

**—JEAN BARCROFT** LAKE ODESSA, MI

**START TO FINISH:** 25 MIN.
**MAKES:** 2 SERVINGS

- 2  haddock or cod fillet (6 ounces each)
  Salt and pepper to taste
- 2/3  cup seasoned bread crumbs
- 2  tablespoons shredded cheddar cheese
- 2  tablespoons butter, melted
- 1½  teaspoons minced fresh parsley
- ¼  teaspoon dried marjoram
- ⅛  teaspoon garlic powder
- ⅛  teaspoon dried rosemary, crushed

Place fish fillets on a greased baking sheet; season with salt and pepper. In a small bowl, combine the remaining ingredients; pat onto the fillets. Bake at 400° for 15-20 minutes or until the fish flakes easily with a fork.

**NUTRITION FACTS** 1 fillet equals 422 cal., 17 g fat (9 g sat. fat), 136 mg chol., 813 mg sodium, 27 g carb. (1 g sugars, 1 g fiber), 39 g pro.

# Homemade Fish Sticks

Moist inside and crunchy outside, these fish sticks are wonderful with oven fries or roasted veggies and a low-fat homemade tartar sauce.

**—JENNIFER ROWLAND** ELIZABETHTOWN, KY

**START TO FINISH:** 25 MIN.
**MAKES:** 2 SERVINGS

½ cup dry bread crumbs
½ teaspoon salt
½ teaspoon paprika
½ teaspoon lemon-pepper seasoning
½ cup all-purpose flour
1 large egg, beaten
¾ pound cod fillets, cut into 1-inch strips
Butter-flavored cooking spray

**1.** Preheat oven to 400°. In a shallow bowl, mix bread crumbs and seasonings. Place flour and egg in separate shallow bowls. Dip each piece of fish in the flour to coat both sides; shake off excess. Dip in the egg, then in the crumb mixture, patting to help the coating adhere.

**2.** Place the fish on a baking sheet coated with cooking spray; spritz with butter-flavored cooking spray. Bake 10-12 minutes or until the fish just begins to flake easily with a fork, turning once.

**NUTRITION FACTS** 1 serving equals 278 cal., 4 g fat (1 g sat. fat), 129 mg chol., 718 mg sodium, 25 g carb. (2 g sugars, 1 g fiber), 33 g pro. *Diabetic Exchanges:* 4 lean meat, 1½ starch.

**Fresh Corn & Tomato Fettuccine, p. 264**

# Meatless for Two

If you've cut meat out of your menu, these dishes are just right. Pasta, salads, sandwiches, pizzas, casseroles and more—all bursting with flavor!

**Personal Veggie Pizzas, p. 279**

**Philly Cheese Fakes, p. 259**

**Creamy Pasta Primavera, p. 256**

## FAST FIX ▸

# Creamy Pasta Primavera

When I think about springtime, asparagus comes to mind. This pasta dish is a wonderful blend of tender, crisp colorful vegetables and a creamy Parmesan cheese sauce.

**—DARLENE BRENDEN** SALEM, OR

**START TO FINISH:** 30 MIN.
**MAKES:** 2 SERVINGS

- 2/3 cup gemelli or spiral pasta
- 6 ounces fresh asparagus, trimmed and cut into 2-inch pieces
- 1 medium carrot, julienned
- 1 teaspoon canola oil
- 2/3 cup cherry tomatoes, halved
- 1 small garlic clove, minced
- 2 tablespoons grated Parmesan cheese
- 2 tablespoons heavy whipping cream
  Dash pepper

1. Cook pasta according to package directions. In a large skillet, saute asparagus and carrots in oil until crisp-tender. Add tomatoes and garlic; cook 1 minute longer.

2. Stir in cheese, cream and pepper. Drain the pasta; toss with asparagus mixture.

**NUTRITION FACTS** 1 1/3 cups equals 260 cal., 10 g fat (5 g sat. fat), 25 mg chol., 114 mg sodium, 35 g carb. (5 g sugars, 3 g fiber), 9 g pro.

## TOP TIP

To trim asparagus, snap off the stalk ends as far down as they will easily break when gently bent, or cut off the tough white portion. You can keep asparagus fresh for a few days by standing it on end in a glass with about 1 in. of water, and setting the glass in the refrigerator.

# Philly Cheese Fakes

Savory mushrooms are the key to this twist on the popular Philly cheese steak sandwich—a nice meatless meal option that's satisfying and tasty.

—**VERONICA VICHIT-VADAKAN** PORTLAND, OR

---

**PREP:** 30 MIN. • **BROIL:** 5 MIN.
**MAKES:** 2 SERVINGS

---

|       |                                      |
|-------|--------------------------------------|
| 2     | tablespoons lemon juice              |
| 2     | garlic cloves, minced                |
| 1½    | teaspoons olive oil                  |
| ¼     | teaspoon smoked paprika              |
| ⅛     | teaspoon salt                        |
| ⅛     | teaspoon pepper                      |
| ½     | pound sliced fresh shiitake mushrooms |
| 1     | medium green pepper, sliced          |
| ¼     | cup thinly sliced onion              |
| 2     | hoagie buns, split                   |
| 2     | slices reduced-fat provolone cheese  |

**1.** In a small bowl, whisk the first six ingredients. In a large bowl, combine mushrooms, green pepper and onion. Pour the dressing over the vegetables; toss to coat.

**2.** Transfer to a 15x10x1-in. baking pan coated with cooking spray. Bake at 450° for 15-20 minutes or until crisp-tender, stirring once.

**3.** Divide the mushroom mixture between bun bottoms and top with cheese. Broil bun halves 3-4 in. from the heat for 2-3 minutes or until the plain bun halves are toasted and the cheese is melted.

**NUTRITION FACTS** 1 sandwich equals 344 cal., 12 g fat (4 g sat. fat), 10 mg chol., 681 mg sodium, 47 g carb. (9 g sugars, 4 g fiber), 17 g pro.

# Tomato Onion Quiche

This scaled-down quiche fills a 7-inch pie pan to the brim and is perfect for serving two or three. I think it's best fresh out of the oven when the cheese is wonderfully gooey.
—**SHERRI CREWS** ST. AUGUSTINE, FL

**PREP:** 20 MIN. • **BAKE:** 45 MIN. + STANDING
**MAKES:** 3 SERVINGS

- 1 sheet refrigerated pie pastry
- 1 cup shredded part-skim mozzarella cheese
- 1/2 cup sliced sweet onion
- 2 small plum tomatoes, seeded and thinly sliced
- 3 medium fresh mushrooms, thinly sliced
- 1/4 cup shredded Parmesan cheese
- 3 large eggs
- 1/2 cup half-and-half cream
- 1/2 teaspoon ground mustard
- 1/2 teaspoon dried basil
- 1/2 teaspoon dried oregano
- 1/2 teaspoon dried thyme

**1.** Cut pastry sheet in half. Repackage and refrigerate one half for another use. On a lightly floured surface, roll out the remaining half into an 8-in. circle. Transfer to a 7-in. pie plate; flute edges.

**2.** Layer half of the mozzarella cheese, onion and tomatoes in the pastry. Top with mushrooms; layer with remaining mozzarella cheese, onion and tomatoes. Sprinkle with Parmesan cheese. In a small bowl, combine eggs, cream, mustard and herbs; pour over top.

**3.** Bake at 350° for 45-55 minutes or until a knife inserted near the center comes out clean. Let stand for 10 minutes before cutting.

**NUTRITION FACTS** 1 serving equals 436 cal., 26 g fat (13 g sat. fat), 265 mg chol., 516 mg sodium, 26 g carb. (7 g sugars, 2 g fiber), 22 g pro.

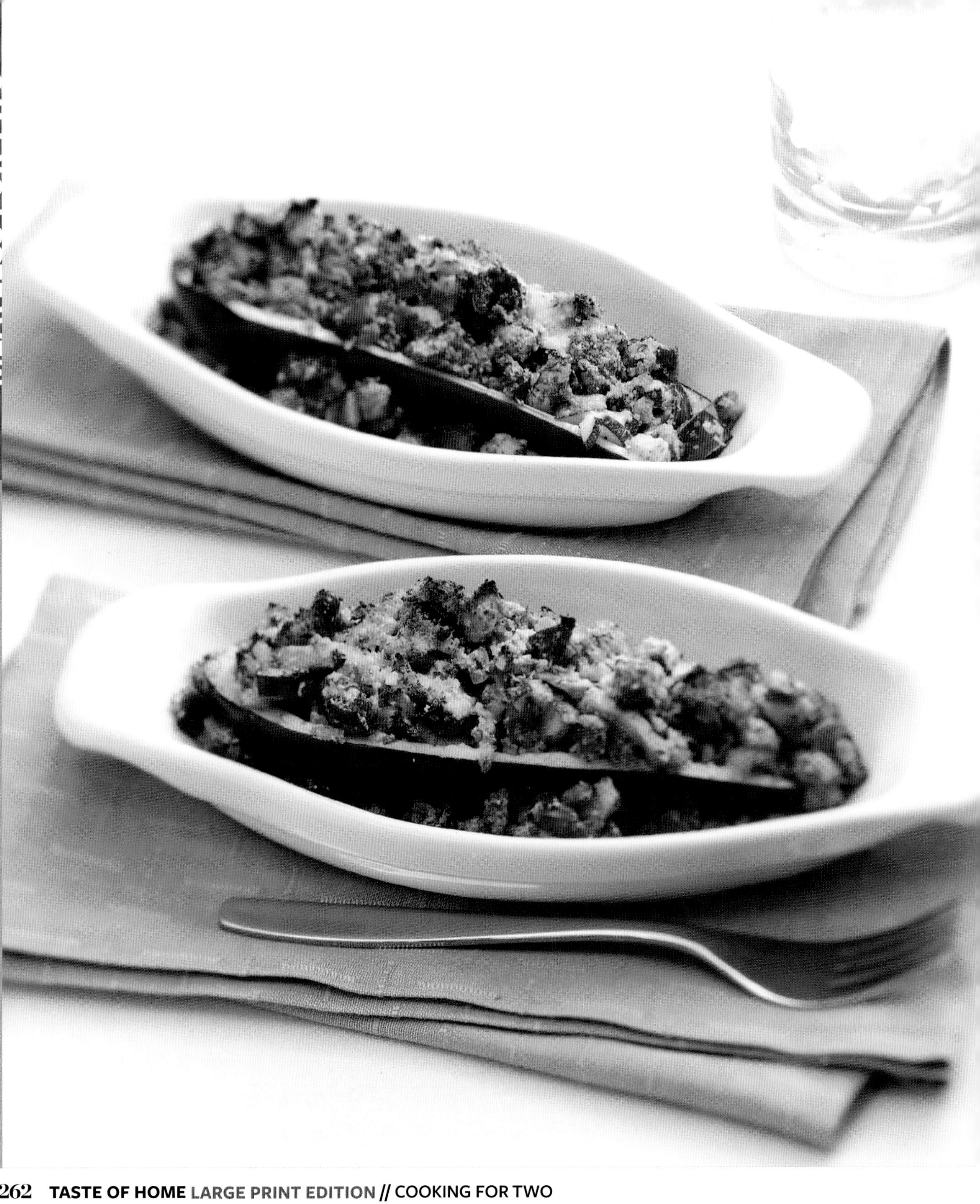

# Veggie-Stuffed Eggplant

Mushrooms, zucchini, peppers and more—this hearty and nutritious dish is loaded with a ton of tasty vegetables.

**—RUBY WILLIAMS** BOGALUSA, LA

---

**PREP:** 25 MIN. • **BAKE:** 20 MIN.
**MAKES:** 2 SERVINGS

---

- 1  medium eggplant
- 1/2  cup chopped onion
- 2  garlic cloves, minced
- 1/2  cup chopped fresh mushrooms
- 1/2  cup chopped zucchini
- 1/2  cup chopped sweet red pepper
- 3/4  cup seeded chopped tomatoes
- 1/4  cup toasted wheat germ
- 2  tablespoons minced fresh parsley
- 1/2  teaspoon dried thyme
- 1/4  teaspoon salt
- 1/4  teaspoon pepper
    Dash crushed red pepper flakes
- 1  tablespoon grated Parmesan cheese

**1.** Cut eggplant in half lengthwise; remove pulp, leaving a 1/4-in.-thick shell. Cube pulp; set shells and pulp aside.

**2.** In a large nonstick skillet coated with cooking spray, saute onion and garlic until the onion is tender. Add mushrooms, zucchini, red pepper and eggplant pulp; saute for 4-6 minutes or until the vegetables are crisp-tender. Stir in tomatoes, wheat germ, parsley, thyme, salt, pepper and pepper flakes; cook for 1 minute.

**3.** Divide the vegetable mixture evenly between the eggplant shells; sprinkle with Parmesan cheese. Place on a baking sheet. Bake at 400° for 20-25 minutes or until the shells are tender.

**NUTRITION FACTS** 1 eggplant half equals 186 cal., 3 g fat (1 g sat. fat), 2 mg chol., 363 mg sodium, 35 g carb. (16 g sugars, 12 g fiber), 11 g pro. *Diabetic Exchanges:* 2 starch, 1 vegetable.

## FAST FIX ▶

# Fresh Corn & Tomato Fettuccine

This recipe combines delicious whole wheat pasta with the best fresh garden produce. It's tossed with heart-healthy olive oil, and a little feta cheese gives it bite.

—**ANGELA SPENGLER** TAMPA, FL

---

**START TO FINISH:** 30 MIN.
**MAKES:** 2 SERVINGS

---

| | |
|---|---|
| 4 | ounces uncooked fettuccine |
| 1 | medium ear sweet corn, husk removed |
| 1 | tablespoon plus 2 teaspoons olive oil, divided |
| 1/4 | cup chopped sweet red pepper |
| 2 | green onions, chopped |
| 1 | cup halved grape tomatoes or chopped tomatoes |
| 1/4 | teaspoon salt |
| 1/2 | teaspoon pepper |
| 1/2 | cup crumbled feta cheese |
| 2 | tablespoons minced fresh parsley |

**1.** In a Dutch oven, cook fettuccine according to package directions, adding corn during the last 8 minutes of cooking.

**2.** Meanwhile, in a small skillet, heat 1 tablespoon oil over medium-high heat. Add red pepper and green onions; cook and stir until tender.

**3.** Drain the pasta and corn; transfer the pasta to a large bowl. Cool corn slightly; cut corn from cob and add to the pasta. Add tomatoes, salt, pepper, the remaining oil and the red pepper mixture; toss to combine. Sprinkle with cheese and parsley.

**NUTRITION FACTS** 2 cups equals 433 cal., 16 g fat (5 g sat. fat), 15 mg chol., 600 mg sodium, 55 g carb. (8 g sugars, 6 g fiber), 16 g pro.

## Meatless Enchilada Bake

I've had this budget-friendly vegetarian recipe for years. You'll enjoy the delicious Tex-Mex flavors, even without the meat.
—**BARBARA STELLUTO** DEVON, PA

**PREP:** 20 MIN. • **BAKE:** 20 MIN. + STANDING
**MAKES:** 3 SERVINGS

- 1   cup shredded zucchini
- 1   tablespoon finely chopped sweet red pepper
- 1   teaspoon olive oil
- 1   garlic clove, minced
- 3/4   cup frozen corn
- 3/4   cup black beans, rinsed and drained
- 1/8   teaspoon salt
- 1/8   teaspoon ground cumin
- 3/4   cup salsa
- 2   tablespoons minced fresh cilantro
- 3   corn tortillas (6 inches)
- 3/4   cup shredded cheddar cheese
      Sour cream, optional

**1.** In a large skillet, saute zucchini and red pepper in oil until the pepper is crisp-tender. Add garlic; cook 1 minute longer. Add corn, beans, salt and cumin; saute 2-3 minutes longer. Stir in salsa and minced cilantro.

**2.** Place a tortilla in the bottom of a 1 1/2-qt. round baking dish coated with cooking spray. Spread with 2/3 cup of the vegetable mixture; sprinkle with 1/4 cup cheese. Repeat layers twice.

**3.** Bake, uncovered, at 350° for 20-25 minutes or until heated through and the cheese is melted. Let stand for 10 minutes before serving. Serve with sour cream if desired.

**NUTRITION FACTS** 1 serving (calculated without sour cream) equals 286 cal., 11 g fat (6 g sat. fat), 30 mg chol., 676 mg sodium, 37 g carb. (4 g sugars, 5 g fiber), 12 g pro. *Diabetic Exchanges:* 2 starch, 2 fat, 1 lean meat.

FAST FIX ▶

## Swiss Macaroni and Cheese

Whenever we visited my husband's good friend, his wife made this dish. I was too shy to ask for the recipe, so I came up with this one. It's very creamy and rich, with a mild Swiss cheese flavor.

—**KATERI SCOTT** AMSTERDAM, NY

**START TO FINISH:** 20 MIN.
**MAKES:** 2 SERVINGS

¾  cup uncooked elbow macaroni
2  tablespoons chopped onion
2  tablespoons butter
1  tablespoon all-purpose flour
1  cup fat-free milk
1  cup shredded Swiss cheese
¼  teaspoon salt
⅛  teaspoon pepper

**1.** Cook macaroni according to package directions. Meanwhile, in a small saucepan, saute onion in butter until tender. Stir in flour until smooth; gradually add milk. Bring to a boil; cook and stir for 2 minutes or until thickened.

**2.** Add cheese, salt and pepper. Drain the macaroni. Add to the cheese mixture; toss gently to coat.

**NUTRITION FACTS** 1 cup equals 464 cal., 27 g fat (17 g sat. fat), 82 mg chol., 569 mg sodium, 32 g carb. (9 g sugars, 1 g fiber), 24 g pro.

## Slow Cooker Veggie Lasagna

Here's a veggie-licious alternative to traditional baked lasagna. I suggest using chunky spaghetti sauce.

**—LAURA DAVISTER** LITTLE SUAMICO, WI

**PREP:** 25 MIN. • **COOK:** 3½ HOURS
**MAKES:** 2 SERVINGS

- ½ cup shredded part-skim mozzarella cheese
- 3 tablespoons 1% cottage cheese
- 2 tablespoons grated Parmesan cheese
- 2 tablespoons egg substitute
- ½ teaspoon Italian seasoning
- ⅛ teaspoon garlic powder
- ¾ cup meatless spaghetti sauce
- ½ cup sliced zucchini
- 2 no-cook lasagna noodles
- 4 cups fresh baby spinach
- ½ cup sliced fresh mushrooms

**1.** In a small bowl, combine the first six ingredients. Spread 1 tablespoon spaghetti sauce on the bottom of a 1½-qt. slow cooker coated with cooking spray. Top with half of the zucchini and a third of the cheese mixture.

**2.** Break noodles into 1-in. pieces; sprinkle half of the noodles over the cheese mixture in the slow cooker. Spread with 1 tablespoon sauce. Top with half the spinach and half the mushrooms. Repeat layers. Top with the remaining cheese mixture and spaghetti sauce.

**3.** Cover and cook on low 3½-4 hours or until the noodles are tender.

**NUTRITION FACTS** 1 serving equals 249 cal., 7 g fat (4 g sat. fat), 22 mg chol., 792 mg sodium, 28 g carb. (10 g sugars, 4 g fiber), 19 g pro. *Diabetic Exchanges:* 2 medium-fat meat, 1½ starch, 1 vegetable.

**DID YOU KNOW?**

If you don't have any Italian seasoning on hand, you can substitute ¼ teaspoon each of basil, thyme, rosemary and oregano for each teaspoon of Italian seasoning called for in a recipe.

**FAST FIX**

## Pronto Vegetarian Peppers

In the summer, I serve these peppers with salad and a roll. At the end of summer, I make and freeze them for cold months when produce costs are high. On a cold day, I love to serve them with a side of warm pasta tossed in olive oil.

**—RENEE HOLLOBAUGH** ALTOONA, PA

**START TO FINISH:** 25 MIN.
**MAKES:** 2 SERVINGS

- 2    large sweet red peppers
- 1    cup canned stewed tomatoes
- 1/3   cup instant brown rice
- 2    tablespoons hot water
- 3/4   cup canned kidney beans, rinsed and drained
- 1/2   cup frozen corn, thawed
- 2    green onions, thinly sliced
- 1/8   teaspoon crushed red pepper flakes
- 1/2   cup shredded part-skim mozzarella cheese
- 1    tablespoon grated Parmesan cheese

**1.** Cut peppers in half lengthwise; remove seeds. Place the peppers in an ungreased shallow microwave-safe dish. Cover and microwave on high for 3-4 minutes or until tender.

**2.** Combine tomatoes, rice and water in a small microwave-safe bowl. Cover and microwave on high for 5-6 minutes or until the rice is tender. Stir in beans, corn, onions and pepper flakes; spoon into the peppers.

**3.** Sprinkle with cheeses. Microwave, uncovered, for 3-4 minutes or until heated through.

**NOTE** This recipe was tested in a 1,100-watt microwave.

**NUTRITION FACTS** 2 stuffed pepper halves equals 341 cal., 7 g fat (3 g sat. fat), 19 mg chol., 556 mg sodium, 56 g carb. (16 g sugars, 11 g fiber), 19 g pro.

# Creamy Broccoli Cauliflower Lasagna

You'll both be eyeing the extra serving of this delicious dish. I use convenient no-cook noodles and frozen vegetables to prepare this easy meatless entree.

**—SUSAN MASIROVITS** JEFFERSON, OH

**PREP:** 20 MIN. • **BAKE:** 35 MIN.
**MAKES:** 3 SERVINGS

- ½ cup grated Parmesan cheese, divided
- ⅓ cup ricotta cheese
- ⅓ cup mayonnaise
- 2 tablespoons 2% milk
- ½ teaspoon dried basil
- ½ teaspoon dried thyme
- ⅛ teaspoon salt
- ⅛ teaspoon pepper
- 3 no-cook lasagna noodles
- 2 cups chopped frozen broccoli-cauliflower blend
- ¼ cup shredded part-skim mozzarella cheese

**1.** In a small bowl, combine 2 tablespoons of the Parmesan cheese, ricotta cheese, mayonnaise, milk, basil, thyme, salt and pepper. Spread ¼ cup into an 8x4-in. loaf pan coated with cooking spray.

**2.** Layer with one noodle, ¼ cup of cheese mixture, 1 cup of vegetable blend and 2 tablespoons Parmesan cheese. Repeat layers. Top with the third noodle and the remaining cheese mixture. Sprinkle with mozzarella and remaining Parmesan.

**3.** Cover and bake at 400° for 25 minutes. Uncover; bake 10-13 minutes longer or until golden brown and bubbly.

**NUTRITION FACTS** 1 serving equals 307 cal., 16 g fat (6 g sat. fat), 33 mg chol., 660 mg sodium, 25 g carb. (7 g sugars, 4 g fiber), 15 g pro.

**TOP TIP**

If you like, you can add more veggies to this dish by substituting eggplant slices for the lasagna noodles. Slice the eggplant lengthwise and layer the slices with the cheese mixture.

EAT SMART

## Three-Cheese Stuffed Shells

Need a great-tasting meatless dish you can count on? These pleasing pasta shells are packed with veggies, three kinds of cheese and wonderful flavor.

**—SHARON DELANEY-CHRONIS**

SOUTH MILWAUKEE, WI

**PREP:** 20 MIN. • **BAKE:** 35 MIN.
**MAKES:** 2 SERVINGS

- 6 uncooked jumbo pasta shells
- 2/3 cup reduced-fat ricotta cheese
- 1/2 cup shredded part-skim mozzarella cheese, divided
- 1/4 cup shredded carrot
- 1/4 cup shredded zucchini
- 2 tablespoons grated Parmesan cheese
- 1/2 teaspoon dried parsley flakes
- 1/2 teaspoon dried oregano
- 1/8 teaspoon garlic powder
- 1/8 teaspoon pepper
- 3/4 cup meatless spaghetti sauce, divided

**1.** Cook pasta according to package directions. Meanwhile, in a small bowl, combine the ricotta, 1/4 cup mozzarella, carrot, zucchini, Parmesan, parsley, oregano, garlic powder and pepper.

**2.** Spread 1/4 cup spaghetti sauce in a 3-cup baking dish coated with cooking spray. Drain the shells; stuff with the cheese mixture. Place in the prepared baking dish. Top with the remaining spaghetti sauce.

**3.** Cover and bake at 350° for 25 minutes. Uncover; sprinkle with the remaining mozzarella. Bake 10-15 minutes longer or until bubbly.

**NUTRITION FACTS** 1 serving equals 326 cal., 10 g fat (6 g sat. fat), 40 mg chol., 721 mg sodium, 37 g carb. (13 g sugars, 3 g fiber), 21 g pro. *Diabetic Exchanges:* 2 medium-fat meat, 2 vegetable, 1 1/2 starch.

## Personal Veggie Pizzas

My mom and I like healthy eating—so this fresh, delicious pizza is our favorite. The assorted veggies and crisp, golden crust are so tasty, no one will miss the sauce.
—**AMBER GERRITY** WEST SENECA, NY

**PREP:** 25 MIN. • **BAKE:** 15 MIN.
**MAKES:** 2 SERVINGS

- 1 package (6½ ounces) pizza crust mix
- 2 tablespoons olive oil
- 2 garlic cloves, minced
- ½ teaspoon dried oregano
- ¼ teaspoon salt
- ¼ teaspoon pepper
- 2 tablespoons grated Parmesan cheese
- 1 plum tomato, thinly sliced
- ¼ cup crumbled tomato and basil feta cheese
- 1 cup shredded part-skim mozzarella cheese
- ¼ cup chopped sweet onion
- ¾ cup sliced fresh mushrooms
- ¼ cup chopped fresh or frozen chopped broccoli
- ¼ to ½ teaspoon crushed red pepper flakes

**1.** Prepare crust mix according to package directions. Divide the dough in half; press each half into a 7-in. circle on a greased baking sheet. Build up edges slightly.

**2.** In a small bowl, combine oil, garlic, oregano, salt, and pepper; spread over the crusts. Sprinkle with Parmesan cheese. Top with tomato, feta, mozzarella, onion, mushrooms, broccoli and pepper flakes.

**3.** Bake at 450° for 12-15 minutes or until the crust is golden brown and the cheese is melted.

**NUTRITION FACTS** 1 pizza equals 669 cal., 28 g fat (10 g sat. fat), 45 mg chol., 1276 mg sodium, 72 g carb. (8 g sugars, 4 g fiber), 30 g pro.

## Portobello Burgers

Robust portobello mushrooms have quite a meaty flavor, so they make the perfect hamburger substitute.

**—THERESA SABBAGH** WINSTON-SALEM, NC

**PREP:** 10 MIN. + STANDING • **GRILL:** 15 MIN.
**MAKES:** 2 SERVINGS

- 2 tablespoons balsamic vinegar
- 1 tablespoon olive oil
- 3 garlic cloves, minced
- 1½ teaspoons minced fresh basil or ½ teaspoon dried basil
- 1½ teaspoons minced fresh oregano or ½ teaspoon dried oregano
  Dash salt
  Dash pepper
- 2 large portobello mushrooms, stems removed
- 2 slices reduced-fat provolone cheese
- 2 hamburger buns, split
- 2 lettuce leaves
- 2 slices tomato

**1.** In a small bowl, whisk the first seven ingredients. Add mushrooms; let stand for 15 minutes, turning twice. Drain the mushrooms; reserve marinade.

**2.** On a greased grill rack, grill the mushrooms, covered, over medium heat or broil 4 in. from the heat for 6-8 minutes on each side or until tender, basting with the reserved marinade. Top with cheese during the last 2 minutes.

**3.** Serve on buns with lettuce and tomato.

**NUTRITION FACTS** 1 burger equals 280 cal., 13 g fat (3 g sat. fat), 10 mg chol., 466 mg sodium, 31 g carb. (8 g sugars, 3 g fiber), 11 g pro. *Diabetic Exchanges:* 2 starch, 1½ fat, 1 medium-fat meat, 1 vegetable.

**Citrus Cream Tartlets, p. 301**

# Desserts for Two

Treat your sweet tooth without the temptation of a whole cake's worth of leftovers! These exquisite sweets are perfect for two.

**Contest-Winning
Easy Tiramisu, p. 298**

**Rustic Fruit
Tart, p. 297**

**Chocolate Turtle
Cheesecake, p. 289**

## Mixed Fruit Shortcakes

This delightful downsized recipe makes two biscuit-like shortcakes. Fill them with fresh fruit of your choice and top with whipped cream for an impressive dinner finale.
—**SUE ROSS** CASA GRANDE, AZ

**START TO FINISH:** 30 MIN. • **MAKES:** 2 SERVINGS

| | |
|---|---|
| 1 | cup mixed fresh berries |
| ½ | cup sliced fresh peaches or nectarines |
| 4 | teaspoons sugar, divided |
| ½ | cup all-purpose flour |
| ¾ | teaspoon baking powder |
| ⅛ | teaspoon salt |
| 2 | tablespoons shortening |
| 3 | tablespoons 2% milk |
| | Whipped cream |

**1.** In a bowl, combine fruit and 2 teaspoons sugar; set aside. In another bowl, combine flour, baking powder and salt; cut in shortening until mixture is crumbly. Stir in milk just until moistened. Drop lightly packed ⅓ cupfuls 2 in. apart on an ungreased baking sheet. Gently flatten into 2½-in. circles. Sprinkle with remaining sugar.

**2.** Bake at 425° for 10-12 minutes or until golden brown. Remove to a wire rack to cool. Split shortcakes in half horizontally. Spoon fruit onto bottoms; spread whipped cream over fruit and cover with the shortcake tops.

**NUTRITION FACTS** 1 serving equals 329 cal., 13 g fat (3 g sat. fat), 2 mg chol., 311 mg sodium, 48 g carb. (20 g sugars, 5 g fiber), 5 g pro.

**⑤ INGREDIENTS**

# White Chocolate Creme Brulee

If you like classic creme brulee, you have to try this version! Dressed up with white chocolate, it's a special romantic treat.

**—CAROLE RESNICK** CLEVELAND, OH

**PREP:** 15 MIN. • **BAKE:** 50 MIN. + CHILLING
**MAKES:** 2 SERVINGS

- 3   large egg yolks
- 6   tablespoons sugar, divided
- 1   cup heavy whipping cream
- 2   ounces white baking chocolate, finely chopped
- ¼   teaspoon vanilla extract

**1.** In a small bowl, whisk egg yolks and 2 tablespoons sugar; set aside. In a small saucepan, combine cream, chocolate and 2 tablespoons sugar. Heat over medium-low heat until the chocolate is melted and the mixture is smooth, stirring constantly.

**2.** Remove from the heat. Stir in vanilla. Stir a small amount of the hot filling into the egg yolk mixture; return all to the pan, stirring constantly.

**3.** Pour into two 10-oz. ramekins. Place in a baking pan. Add 1 in. of boiling water to pan. Bake, uncovered, at 325° for 50-55 minutes or until the center is set. Remove from the water bath. Cool for 10 minutes. Refrigerate for at least 4 hours.

**4.** If using a creme brulee torch, sprinkle the custards with the remaining sugar. Heat the sugar with the torch until caramelized. Serve immediately.

**5.** If broiling the custards, place the ramekins on a baking sheet; let stand at room temperature for 15 minutes. Sprinkle with the remaining sugar. Broil 8 in. from the heat for 4-7 minutes or until the sugar is caramelized. Refrigerate for 1-2 hours or until firm.

**NUTRITION FACTS** 1 serving equals 854 cal., 62 g fat (36 g sat. fat), 488 mg chol., 86 mg sodium, 70 g carb. (68 g sugars, 0 fiber), 9 g pro.

DESSERTS FOR TWO

# Chocolate Turtle Cheesecake

I always get compliments whenever I whip up this rich little cheesecake. With layers of caramel, chocolate and vanilla, it's an instant classic!

**—ERIN BYRD** SPRINGFIELD, MO

---

**PREP:** 20 MIN. • **BAKE:** 20 MIN. + CHILLING
**MAKES:** 2 SERVINGS

---

- 1/3 cup crushed vanilla wafers (about 10 wafers)
- 4 teaspoons butter, melted
- 4 ounces cream cheese, softened
- 2 tablespoons sugar
- 1/2 teaspoon vanilla extract
- 2 tablespoons beaten egg
- 2 tablespoons hot fudge ice cream topping, warmed
- 1 tablespoon caramel ice cream topping, warmed

**1.** In a small bowl, combine wafer crumbs and butter. Press mixture onto the bottom and 1/2 in. up the sides of a greased 4-in. springform pan.

**2.** In a small bowl, beat cream cheese, sugar and vanilla until smooth. Add egg; beat on low speed just until combined. Spread half of the mixture into the crust. Stir fudge topping into the remaining batter; gently spread over the cream cheese layer. Place pan on a baking sheet.

**3.** Bake at 350° for 20-25 minutes or until center is almost set. Cool on a wire rack for 10 minutes. Carefully run a knife around the edge of the pan to loosen; cool 1 hour longer.

**4.** Refrigerate overnight. Remove the sides of the pan. Drizzle caramel topping over cheesecake.

**NUTRITION FACTS** 1/2 cheesecake equals 510 cal., 33 g fat (19 g sat. fat), 150 mg chol., 362 mg sodium, 47 g carb. (27 g sugars, 1 g fiber), 8 g pro.

# Cornflake Fried Ice Cream

Make this Mexican restaurant-style dessert at home! Drizzle hot fudge or caramel on top of this crunchy, creamy frozen treat.

**—RONDA WEIRICH** PLAINS, KS

**PREP:** 20 MIN. + FREEZING
**MAKES:** 2 SERVINGS

- 1 cup vanilla ice cream
- ¼ cup heavy whipping cream, divided
- ¼ teaspoon vanilla extract, divided
- ¾ cup crushed frosted cornflakes
- ¼ teaspoon ground cinnamon
  Oil for deep-fat frying
  Whipped cream

**1.** Using a ½-cup ice cream scoop, form two balls of ice cream. Cover and freeze for 1 hour or until firm. In a small bowl, whisk 2 tablespoons cream and ⅛ teaspoon vanilla. In a shallow bowl, combine cornflakes and cinnamon. Dip ice cream balls into the cream mixture, then roll in the cornflakes. Set aside the remaining cornflakes. Cover the ice cream balls and freeze for 1 hour or until firm.

**2.** In a small bowl, whisk together the remaining cream and vanilla. Dip ice cream balls into cream mixture, then roll in the remaining cereal mixture. Cover and freeze for 1 hour or until firm.

**3.** In an electric skillet or deep-fat fryer, heat oil to 375°. Fry each ice cream ball for 12-15 seconds or until golden. Drain on paper towels. Serve immediately with whipped cream.

**NUTRITION FACTS** 1 ice cream ball equals 323 cal., 22 g fat (12 g sat. fat), 70 mg chol., 138 mg sodium, 31 g carb. (18 g sugars, 1 g fiber), 3 g pro.

# Coffee Cream Tortilla Cups

Here's a special dessert for two. Crispy tortilla bowls hold creamy coffee-flavored pudding topped with a colorful mix of fresh berries.

**—AMBER ZURBRUGG** ALLIANCE, OH

**PREP:** 15 MIN. + CHILLING • **BAKE:** 10 MIN.
**MAKES:** 2 SERVINGS

- 2   flour tortillas (8 inches), warmed
- 1   tablespoon butter, melted
- 1   tablespoon sugar
- ½   teaspoon ground cinnamon
- ½   cup half and half cream
- 2   teaspoons instant coffee granules
- 5   tablespoons instant French vanilla pudding mix
- 1   cup whipped topping
- 1½  cups fresh blueberries, raspberries and sliced strawberries

1. Brush one side of each tortilla with butter. Gently press each into a 10-oz. custard cup, buttered side up; pleat edges. Combine sugar and cinnamon; sprinkle over tortillas. Bake at 400° for 8-10 minutes or until crisp and lightly browned. Cool on a wire rack.

2. In a small bowl, combine the cream and coffee granules until dissolved. Add pudding mix; whisk for 2 minutes. Let stand for 2 minutes or until soft-set. Fold in whipped topping. Cover and refrigerate for 1 hour. Spoon into tortilla cups. Top with berries.

**NUTRITION FACTS** 1 serving equals 548 cal., 21 g fat (14 g sat. fat), 45 mg chol., 638 mg sodium, 79 g carb. (39 g sugars, 3 g fiber), 7 g pro.

**TOP TIP**

Once you've mastered the trick of making tortilla cups, let yourself play with the fillings! Swap out the pudding for tangy lemon curd, or use a different flavor of pudding. Chocolate would mix especially well with the coffee flavor and raspberries.

EAT SMART FAST FIX

# Meringues with Fresh Berries

Juicy ripe berries and a dollop of light cream fill these cloud-like meringue desserts. I double this recipe when we have friends over for dinner, and they always rave about it.
—**AGNES WARD** STRATFORD, ON

**PREP:** 20 MIN. • **BAKE:** 1 HOUR + COOLING
**MAKES:** 2 SERVINGS

- 2 large egg whites
- 1/8 teaspoon cream of tartar
  Dash salt
- 1/4 cup sugar
- 1/4 teaspoon vanilla extract
- 1 cup mixed fresh berries
- 1/2 teaspoon sugar, optional
- 1/3 cup sour cream
- 1/8 to 1/4 teaspoon rum extract

**1.** Place egg whites in a small bowl; let stand at room temperature for 30 minutes. Add cream of tartar and salt; beat on medium speed until soft peaks form. Gradually beat in sugar, 1 tablespoon at a time, on high until stiff peaks form. Beat in vanilla.

**2.** Drop the meringue into two mounds on a parchment paper-lined baking sheet. Use the back of a spoon to shape the mounds into 3½-in. cups.

**3.** Bake at 225° for 1-1¼ hours or until the meringues are set and dry. Turn oven off; leave the meringues in the oven for 1 hour. Remove to wire racks to cool.

**4.** In a small bowl, combine berries and, if desired, sugar; let stand for 5 minutes. Combine sour cream and extract; spoon into the meringue shells. Top with the berries.

**NUTRITION FACTS** 1 serving equals 222 cal., 7 g fat (5 g sat. fat), 27 mg chol., 149 mg sodium, 33 g carb. (30 g sugars, 2 g fiber), 5 g pro. *Diabetic Exchanges:* 2 starch, 1½ fat, ½ fruit.

# Rustic Fruit Tart

My husband and I love pie, but we can't eat a whole 9-inch pie by ourselves. So I make these easy tarts using rhubarb and raspberries picked at home. Sometimes I substitute apples, peaches or blueberries for the rhubarb.

—**NAOMI OLSON** HAMILTON, MI

**PREP:** 20 MIN. + STANDING • **BAKE:** 25 MIN.
**MAKES:** 2 SERVINGS

- 1   cup all-purpose flour
- ½   teaspoon salt
- ¼   cup canola oil
- 2   tablespoons milk
- 1   cup diced fresh or frozen rhubarb, thawed
- 1   cup fresh or frozen raspberries, thawed
- ½   cup sugar
- 2   tablespoons quick-cooking tapioca

**GLAZE**

- 6   tablespoons confectioners' sugar
- 1   teaspoon water
- ⅛   teaspoon almond extract

**1.** In a large bowl, combine flour and salt. Add oil and milk, tossing with a fork until the mixture forms a ball. Shape the dough into a disk; wrap in plastic wrap. Refrigerate for at least 1 hour.

**2.** In another bowl, combine rhubarb, raspberries, sugar and tapioca; let stand for 15 minutes. Unwrap the dough and place on a parchment-lined baking sheet. Cover with waxed paper and roll into an 11-in. circle. Discard the waxed paper.

**3.** Spoon fruit mixture into the center of the dough to within 2 in. of the edges. Fold the edges of the dough over the fruit, leaving the center uncovered. Bake at 400° for 25-30 minutes or until the crust is golden brown and the filling is bubbly. Remove to a wire rack. Combine glaze ingredients until smooth. Drizzle over the warm tart.

**NOTE** If using frozen rhubarb, measure it while still frozen, then thaw completely. Drain, but do not press liquid out.

**NUTRITION FACTS** 1 serving equals 852 cal., 30 g fat (2 g sat. fat), 2 mg chol., 602 mg sodium, 141 g carb. (77 g sugars, 7 g fiber), 8 g pro.

**(5) INGREDIENTS** **FAST FIX**

# Contest-Winning Easy Tiramisu

This recipe gives you the taste of traditional tiramisu in an instant. My husband and I love this dish; because he has diabetes, I make it with sugar-free wafers and sugar-free pudding.

**—BETTY CLAYCOMB** ALVERTON, PA

**START TO FINISH:** 10 MIN.
**MAKES:** 2 SERVINGS

| | |
|---|---|
| 14 | vanilla wafers, divided |
| 1 | teaspoon instant coffee granules |
| 2 | tablespoons hot water |
| 2 | snack-size cups (3½ ounces each) vanilla pudding |
| ¼ | cup whipped topping |
| 1 | teaspoon baking cocoa |

**1.** Set aside four vanilla wafers; coarsely crush the remaining wafers. Divide the wafer crumbs between two dessert dishes.

**2.** In a small bowl, dissolve coffee granules in hot water. Drizzle over the wafer crumbs. Spoon pudding into dessert dishes. Top with whipped topping; sprinkle with cocoa. Garnish with the reserved vanilla wafers.

**NUTRITION FACTS** 1 serving equals 267 cal., 9 g fat (4 g sat. fat), 4 mg chol., 219 mg sodium, 41 g carb. (28 g sugars, 1 g fiber), 3 g pro.

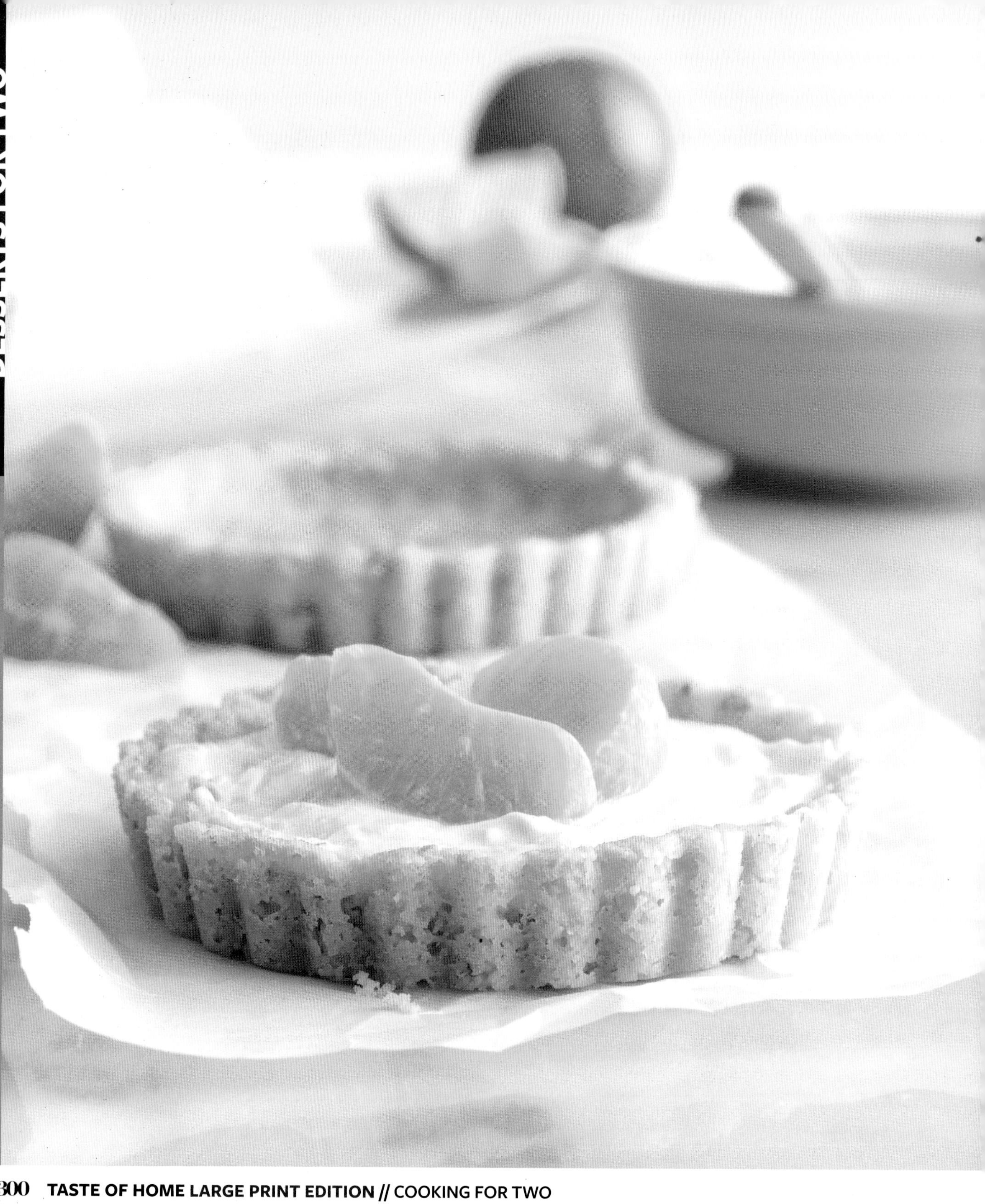

# Citrus Cream Tartlets

This rich, creamy dessert can be made ahead of time.
—**BRIAN BARGER** CHEVY CHASE, MD

---

**PREP:** 20 MIN. • **BAKE:** 15 MIN. + CHILLING
**MAKES:** 2 SERVINGS

---

- ½ cup chopped macadamia nuts, toasted
- 3 tablespoons sugar
- 2 tablespoons all-purpose flour
- 2 tablespoons cold butter
- 6 ounces cream cheese, softened
- ¼ cup confectioners' sugar
- 2 teaspoons each orange, lemon and lime juice
- 1 teaspoon each grated orange, lemon and lime peel

**1.** In a food processor, combine the nuts, sugar and flour; cover and process until blended. Add butter; blend until mixture forms coarse crumbs.

**2.** Press onto the bottom and up the sides of two greased 4-in. tartlet pans with removable bottoms. Bake at 350° for 13-15 minutes or until golden brown. Cool completely.

**3.** In a small bowl, beat cream cheese until fluffy. Add the confectioners' sugar, citrus juices and peels; beat until blended.

**4.** Spoon into crusts. Refrigerate for at least 1 hour.

**NUTRITION FACTS** 1 serving equals 799 cal., 66 g fat (28 g sat. fat), 124 mg chol., 521 mg sodium, 50 g carb. (38 g sugars, 3 g fiber), 9 g pro.

**FAST FIX** ▶

# Chocolate Lava Cakes

Since this dessert is served hot, it can be in the oven while you eat the main course. The recipe can easily be increased to serve any number of chocolate lovers.

—**HEIDI WILCOX** LAPEER, MI

---

**START TO FINISH:** 25 MIN.
**MAKES:** 2 SERVINGS

---

1/3 cup semisweet chocolate chips
1/4 cup butter, cubed
1/3 cup superfine sugar
1 large egg
4½ teaspoons all-purpose flour
1/4 cup white baking chips
    Confectioners' sugar

**1.** Grease the bottom and sides of two 6-oz. ramekins or custard cups. Place ramekins on a baking sheet; set aside.

**2.** In a microwave, melt semisweet chocolate and butter; stir until smooth. Set aside to cool.

**3.** In a small bowl, combine sugar, egg and flour; stir in the chocolate mixture. Fold in white baking chips. Spoon batter into the prepared ramekins.

**4.** Bake at 400° until a thermometer reads 160° and the cake sides are set, about 15-20 minutes. Remove the ramekins to a wire rack to cool for 5 minutes. Invert onto serving plates; dust with confectioners' sugar.

**NUTRITION FACTS** 1 cake equals 635 cal., 40 g fat (24 g sat. fat), 169 mg chol., 219 mg sodium, 68 g carb. (61 g sugars, 2 g fiber), 6 g pro.

# Layered Chocolate Pudding Dessert

This layered dessert is cool, creamy, chocolaty and a winner with everyone who tries it. What's not to like?

—**CARMA BLOSSER** LIVERMORE, CO

**PREP:** 30 MIN. + COOLING
**MAKES:** 2 SERVINGS

- 1/3 cup all-purpose flour
- 3 tablespoons chopped pecans
- 3 tablespoons butter, melted
- 3 ounces cream cheese, softened
- 1/3 cup confectioners' sugar
- 1 cup whipped topping, divided
- 2/3 cup cold 2% milk
- 3 tablespoons instant chocolate pudding mix

**1.** In a small bowl, combine flour, pecans and butter; press into an ungreased 5¾x3x2-in. loaf pan. Bake at 350° for 10-12 minutes or until crust is lightly browned. Cool on a wire rack.

**2.** In a small bowl, beat cream cheese and confectioners' sugar until smooth; fold in ½ cup whipped topping. Spread over crust.

**3.** In a small bowl, whisk milk and pudding mix for 2 minutes. Let stand for 2 minutes or until soft-set. Spread over cream cheese mixture. Spread with remaining whipped topping. Chill until serving.

**NUTRITION FACTS** 1 serving equals 692 cal., 42 g fat (25 g sat. fat), 81 mg chol., 614 mg sodium, 67 g carb. (41 g sugars, 2 g fiber), 11 g pro.

# Blueberry Peach Fool

Usher in warm weather with this creamy whipped dessert. It's filled with fresh, fruity goodness that hints of warm weather and appeals to all ages.

—*TASTE OF HOME* TEST KITCHEN

**PREP:** 25 MIN. + CHILLING
**MAKES:** 2 SERVINGS

1½  cups chopped peeled fresh peaches or frozen unsweetened sliced peaches, thawed and chopped
¼  cup sugar
¼  cup unsweetened apple juice
½  teaspoon ground cinnamon
Dash salt
1  cup heavy whipping cream
¼  teaspoon vanilla extract
1½  cups fresh or frozen blueberries, thawed

**1.** In a small saucepan, combine peaches, sugar, apple juice, cinnamon and salt. Bring to a boil. Reduce heat; cover and simmer for 6-8 minutes or until the peaches are tender. Cool slightly.

**2.** In a blender, process peach mixture until smooth. Transfer to a small bowl; cover and refrigerate until chilled.

**3.** Just before serving, whip cream until it begins to thicken. Add vanilla; beat until soft peaks form. Fold into the peach mixture. In parfait glasses, alternately layer blueberries and the cream mixture.

**NUTRITION FACTS** 1 serving equals 641 cal., 45 g fat (27 g sat. fat), 163 mg chol., 121 mg sodium, 62 g carb. (53 g sugars, 6 g fiber), 4 g pro.

# Mixed Berry Sundaes

These pretty sundaes are an easy way to add fruit and calcium to your diet. Berries star in the dish, which I make as a simple breakfast or healthy dessert for two.
**—EDIE DESPAIN** LOGAN, UT

---

**START TO FINISH:** 10 MIN.
**MAKES:** 2 SERVINGS

---

- ¼ cup halved fresh strawberries
- ¼ cup each fresh raspberries, blueberries and blackberries
- 3 teaspoons honey, divided
- ½ cup fat-free plain Greek yogurt
- 2 tablespoons pomegranate juice
- 2 tablespoons chopped walnuts, toasted

**1.** In a small bowl, combine berries and 1 teaspoon of the honey; spoon the berry mixture into two dessert dishes.

**2.** Combine yogurt, pomegranate juice and the remaining honey; spoon over the berries. Sprinkle with walnuts.

**NUTRITION FACTS** 1 dish equals 160 cal., 5 g fat (0 sat. fat), 0 chol., 33 mg sodium, 22 g carb. (18 g sugars, 3 g fiber), 10 pro. *Diabetic Exchanges:* 1 starch, 1 fat, ½ fruit.

# GENERAL RECIPE INDEX

## FISH (*also see Seafood*)

## (5) INGREDIENTS

Deep-Fried Onions with
  Dipping Sauce, 55
Dill Spiral Bites, 36
Easy Mango Salsa, 56
Fresh Corn & Tomato
  Fettuccine, 264
Meatless Enchilada Bake, 267
Personal Veggie Pizzas, 279
Philly Cheese Fakes for Two, 259
Portobello Burgers, 280
Pronto Vegetarian Peppers, 272
Roasted Tomato Soup with
  Fresh Basil, 86
Spinach-Mushroom
  Scrambled Eggs, 15
Swiss Macaroni and Cheese, 268
Three-Cheese Stuffed Shells, 276
Tomato Onion Quiche, 260
Veggie-Stuffed Eggplant, 263

## MUSHROOMS
Individual Italian Frittatas, 16
Philly Cheese Fakes for Two, 259

Portobello Burgers, 280
Skewerless Stovetop Kabobs, 223
Spinach-Mushroom
  Scrambled Eggs, 15

## MUSTARD
Honey Dijon Pork, 200

## NUTS & PEANUT BUTTER
Almond Cheese Spread, 51
Cashew Chicken, 175
Peanut Butter Oatmeal, 31
Salmon Salad with Glazed
  Walnuts, 229

## OATS & GRANOLA
Flaxseed Oatmeal Pancakes, 24
Peanut Butter Oatmeal, 31

## ONIONS
Deep-Fried Onions with
  Dipping Sauce, 55
Tomato Onion Quiche, 260

## ORANGES
Citrus Cream Tartlets, 301

## PANCAKES & WAFFLES
Flaxseed Oatmeal Pancakes, 24
Fluffy Pumpkin Pancakes, 12

## PASTA & NOODLES
Beef Macaroni Skillet, 156
Chicken Mexican Manicotti, 196
Comforting Tuna Casserole, 230

Creamy Broccoli Cauliflower
  Lasagna, 275
Creamy Pasta Primavera, 256
Favorite Italian Casserole, 211
Fresh Corn & Tomato
  Fettuccine, 264
Greek-Style Ravioli, 148
Ham and Broccoli Linguine, 215
Italian Sausage Minestrone, 77
Pepperoni Lasagna Roll-Ups, 220
Skillet Pasta, 164
Slow Cooker Veggie Lasagna, 271
Swiss Macaroni and Cheese, 268
Tender Beef over Noodles, 152
Thai Chicken Pasta, 172
Three-Cheese Stuffed Shells, 276
Turkey & Bow Ties, 187

## PEACHES
Blueberry Peach Fool, 306

## PEARS
Pear Harvest Salad, 116

## PEAS
Sweet Peas Parma, 128

## PEPPERS & CHILIES
Chicken Chili Enchiladas, 184
Chipotle Smashed Sweet
  Potatoes, 127
Feta Stuffed Peppers, 167
Pepper & Salsa Cod, 246
Pork Burgers with Grilled
  Pineapple & Peppers, 98

# ALPHABETICAL RECIPE INDEX